TEACHING READING TO BLACK ADOLESCENT MALES

TEACHING READING TO BLACK ADOLESCENT MALES

CLOSING THE ACHIEVEMENT GAP

ALFRED W. TATUM

STENHOUSE PUBLISHERS
PORTLAND, MAINE

Stenhouse Publishers
www.stenhouse.com

Credits
Page 30: "We Real Cool" by Gwendolyn Brooks reprinted by consent of Brooks Permissions.
Pages 64–65: Excerpts from the article "Prison Privatisation" are reprinted by permission of corporatewatch.org.
Page 66: "I, Too" by Langston Hughes from *The Collected Poems of Langston Hughes* by Langston Hughes copyright © 1994 by The Estate of Langston Hughes. Used by permission of Alfred A. Knopf, a division of Random House, Inc.
Page 66: "America" by Claude McKay is reprinted by courtesy of the literary representative for the works of Claude McKay, Schomburg Center for Research in Black Culture, The New York Public Library, Astor, Lenox and Tilden Foundations.

Tatum, Alfred W.
    Teaching reading to black adolescent males: closing the achievement
        gap / Alfred W. Tatum. p. cm.
    Includes bibliographical references.
    ISBN 1-57110-393-7
    1. African American boys–Education (Secondary) 2. African American
    teenagers–Education (Secondary) 3. Reading (Secondary)–United
    States. 4. Reading (Remedial teaching)–United States. 5. African
    American boys–Social conditions. 6. African American
    teenagers–Social conditions. I. Title.

LC2779.T38 2006
428.4071'2
                                                            2006044255
Library of Congress Cataloging-in-Publication Data on file.
Cover design by Diana Coe
Interior design by Martha Drury

Manufactured in the United States of America on acid-free paper
12 11 10 09 08   9 8 7 6 5

This book is dedicated to the river and the fire, two thoroughfares of the African American struggle toward liberation in America. It is also dedicated to my sons, Amal-Sundar and Andrew T—the river and the fire.

CONTENTS

ACKNOWLEDGMENTS

A close friend recently asked me, "Did you ever imagine it?" He was wondering whether I had ever envisioned becoming a professor, an education consultant, and a writer. He recalled my passion to teach African American teenagers, particularly males, in the neighborhood where I was raised. I replied that I could never have imagined the good fortune that has come my way. I only wanted to use my heart and my mind to make the world in which I live a better place. In that vein, I acknowledge all those who have nurtured me in both heart and mind. I acknowledge my mother, Karen Tatum, who taught me how to be compassionate and humble. I acknowledge my teachers, who shaped my understanding of the world. I acknowledge all of my former students, who challenged me to become a better teacher. I acknowledge those who have responded to my writing and challenged me to "get it right" so that my words and ideas might make sense to a larger, diverse audience. Foremost among these is William Varner of Stenhouse Publishers, who helped me shape the text that follows. I also acknowledge those who have been patient with me over the years and encouraged me to keep on keeping on at times when I just wanted to rest. I acknowledge Sabrina, my wife of nine years, who believes in me and encourages me to "bring the thunder." She has been with me every step of the way—including the relocations, the late-night writing, the kitchen table conversations, the "please read this and tell me what you think" times, and the take-care-of-the-boys-while-I-finish-my-Ph.D. years. Lastly, I acknowledge my two sons, Amal-Sundar and Andrew T. They are the reason why I stay focused on my passion to address the literacy needs of black males.

INTRODUCTION

My older son was placed at gunpoint for the first time in his life at the age of three—eleven years earlier in his life than my first such experience. Two young black men carjacked my wife and son and demanded money. After she told them she had none, they forced their way into our home. One of them grabbed my wife by her arm, and the other picked up my son, as I have on many occasions. I imagine this embrace felt strangely different to him. The intruders placed my son on the couch near the door, forced my wife upstairs, and proceeded to ransack our house.

I arrived home approximately twenty minutes later. Surprised to see my son sitting downstairs alone at such a late hour—it was after 9:30 p.m.—I called for my wife. Before she could respond, a strange man rushed toward me from the dining room with a long-barreled handgun pointed directly at my head. It took me a minute to realize what was happening. The man with the gun forced me to the floor. As he started to blindfold me, my first thought was to grab him. Then I heard the second man coming down the stairs. I decided to cooperate, hoping that being robbed would be the worst of it.

My son was still sitting on the couch, several feet away from me. "Dad, why are you on the floor?" he asked. I did not answer; I did not know how to react.

"Answer him before I shoot yo' punk ass," I heard one of the intruders say.

I tell my son that I am just playing and that I want him to be quiet until the game is over. I feel my wallet and car keys being pulled from my back pocket. I lay in quiet prayer, contemplating the worst but hoping for the best.

"I know you prayin', ain't you?"

"Yes, sir," I reply, to a man I suspect is ten years my junior.

As they carry things out of our house, I hear one of the men refer to the other by name. This scares me: will they kill me now that I can identify one of them by name? I pray some more, placing my trust in God.

Several minutes go by. Then I hear one of the men order me to stand and take my clothes off. By now my wife is lying beside me. As I undress, she is also told to stand, but to keep her clothes on. I am relieved; had she been forced to take her clothes off, I probably would have hit my breaking point and would have tried to strike back. As it was, standing nude, I never felt so helpless.

We are told to walk up the stairs. I grab my son. As he and my wife walk in front of me, I am sure I'll be shot in the back. One of the intruders follows us up the stairs. He orders us to lie in the bedroom farthest from the stairs and not move for thirty minutes.

I hear the door shut, but I am not certain that the men have left. This may be a trick to see whether I will follow their directions. I listen for the sound of an engine starting or a car driving away, but I hear nothing. I feel more humiliated by the minute because I know that my wife is waiting for me to respond. Several minutes go by before I finally get up, remove the blindfold, and look around. Computers, televisions, artwork, stereo equipment, cameras, video games, and a car are gone, and the phone has been ripped from the wall. But we are alive, and physically unhurt.

The home invasion left none of us unscathed. For several months, my son would not sleep alone in his bedroom. It would take close to two years and a move to a different neighborhood before my wife felt secure again.

This random assault on my family shattered my sense of my role and function in society. After the incident, I felt an extreme inner tension between sticking with my passion and letting it go. I was concerned with empowering young black males. I had been writing about the need to restructure educational opportunities that would allow them to have a broader array of options and to participate more fully in American society. Now I was one of their victims. For several days after the home invasion, I had no interest in such things. I even found myself making remarks that would be considered vile and racist. "To hell with them niggers," I said to my wife.

Later, I came to realize how easy it is for others to castigate black males because I was now guilty of doing the same thing. After weeks of reflection, I regained, and even strengthened, my commitment to black males. Two facts brought me back: my two sons are black males, and my life was spared. Several weeks following my experience, I read in the newspaper that the victims of other home invasions were murdered. I feel that I am indebted to my sons and to the higher power that allowed me to live. Out of that indebtedness, I carry on in my efforts to address issues critical to young black men and their development. I want to publicize the need to reconceptualize the role of literacy in their lives. With renewed energy, with passion and pain, I write. This book is my attempt to speak on behalf of all those young black males who yearn for understanding as they journey through rough terrain. Many of these young men want educators to respond to their needs and so help release them from a poverty-ridden paralysis that stiffens dreams.

In Chapter 1, I describe the changes that take place in adolescence, specifically with regard to black males' literacy development. In Chapter 2, I describe the "turmoil milieu" and its implications for literacy among black males who attend school in America's economically starved urban centers. I consider how personal accounts of turmoil can be used as texts to help teachers open the pipelines of black males' entry into America's mainstream. Chapter 3 is concerned with the reading achievement gap as it relates to black males and how educators must seek comprehensive solutions to address the turmoil that young black men experience in their day-to-day lives. Chapters 4, 5, and 6 focus on the kind of framework young black males need in an educational setting, including concepts of literacy instruction, curriculum orientation, and culturally responsive pedagogy. Chapters 7, 8, and 9 are concerned specifically with literacy instruction for black males. In these chapters I lay out a comprehensive framework for literacy teaching, text discussion, and assessment. In Chapters 10 and 11, I suggest methods of professional development that can help individual teachers improve their own instruction and effectiveness.

I am well aware that a single text does not have the power to do all things. A text not honestly written, however, can do nothing. This book is an honest attempt to strengthen the relationship between literacy and the black male.

CHAPTER 1

LITERACY DEVELOPMENT IN BLACK ADOLESCENT MALES

Let me decide for myself what's to my advantage.

Finally, even if I achieve nothing, even if my reasoning is wrong, even if I break my neck and prove a complete flop, I still don't care; I'll go ahead with my plans because that's the way I want it to be.

Fyodor Dostoevsky, *The Adolescent*

The quotes from Dostoevsky's *The Adolescent* given on the previous page capture the shifts in thinking of Arkady, the title character, as he gropes his way toward manhood. The young man is determined to control his own destiny. Throughout the novel, Arkady seeks answers to "the question." His particular question emerged from the society in which he lived and was influenced by his upbringing as an economically disadvantaged youth abandoned by his father. Several questions of my own came to mind as I read this novel. What is causing Arkady to change his thinking about the world and his place in it? When did the shift from boyhood to manhood begin? How can his growth be supported?

Like Arkady, all adolescent males experience an "adolescent shift"—the transition from childhood to young adulthood. During this time young men begin to exert their own agency to do or not do something. They attempt to define who they are and what they want to become. They begin to form their own ideas about the world and their place within it. Their thinking is largely influenced by the relationships they form and the activities they choose. Although shaped by current circumstances, the adolescent shift can also be shaped by historical events and their residual effects.

THE ADOLESCENT SHIFT AND BLACK MALES

During early adolescence poor black males become aware of the biting divide between how they live and how the rest of American society lives. Also during this period, seeds of despair, crime, joblessness, incarceration, and death take root. It is easy for many young black males to conclude that the world is indifferent to their existence. In the movie *Boyz N the Hood,* Ice Cube, in the role of Doughboy, is given cause to reflect on the poor black male's invisibility. His brother Ricky, a high school football star, is murdered. The following day there is no mention of Ricky's death in the newspaper. Doughboy mentions this and concludes, "Either they don't know, don't show, or don't care about what's going on in the 'hood." Feelings of invisibility as the root cause of many of the black male's problems are a common theme in fiction and nonfiction texts about the lives of black males. These feelings are usually prompted by the individual's assessment of his condition in the society in which he lives. I tried to capture these feelings of invisibility in a poem:

Does the world care if I exist?

Or am I just America's problem?

Don't they know I am dying like no other?

No, they just fear me, they can't hear me

Hell, they'll just lock me up in *juvey* and throw away the key

Man, I can't stand for that

I got to fight back

I'm dying anyway

Might as well take some with me—black, brown, white, don't matter

I'm tired of living in poverty

I get hungry too

You expect me to just watch you eat

While you mistreat me in the schools and in the streets

Hell, you can't even teach me how to read—Mr. and Mrs. Teacher

Then you flunk me, and blame it on me

Some of it's my fault

Probably some is my momma's fault as well

But you're at fault, too

So I'll sling a little to get paid

Get a little respect while I'm at it, maybe get laid

Death don't matter, the way I'm living I feel dead anyway

Tired of being on my *knees* begging

Trying to do the right thing and never getting ahead

My homeboy graduated from high school, now he's dead

It's about living a little now, the only time I know I got for sure

Man, you don't hear me

I can beat drums at your doorstep all night

You'll just say get away with all that Hip-Hop

It is really a cry, a scream for your attention

But my manhood won't let me come right out and ask for help

With your track record, I don't trust that you'll help me anyway.

Why should I put myself out like that?

I don't want your pity, or *your* crying

Teach me how to *man-up,* and be a man

Help me to stop dying

If you don't, this nation will continue to spill over with the black male's
    blood

You'll have to build more jails

There you go—I told you the deal

I spilled my guts
It is now your time to act
If you don't act
I now believe that *America does not care if I exist* is a fact.
No more peace until we all get a piece (American pie)
Damn, my time expired. I'm gone.

This poem was inspired in part by my childhood and the changes I noticed that took place among some of the young black males in my neighborhood as we grew up. Cynicism, self-loathing, despair, a retarded sense of one's destiny, and frustration take on a life of their own when they penetrate black male childhood. Early aspirations wither as many young black men attempt to become one of the "boys" in order to survive.

Black males' adolescent shift is greatly influenced by their schooling and whatever value they attach to it. Anderson Franklin (2004), in *From Brotherhood to Manhood,* explains how feelings of alienation and ambivalence toward formal education are cultivated:

> *What schools often provide for boys of African descent is a slowly nurtured understanding that being somebody is more directly attached to the peer culture than to the classroom. Our potential and ability are robbed by the climate in schools thoughtlessness. . . . Such attitudes cultivated among black males by the school environment play into racially coded expectations that become a self-fulfilling prophecy. Poorly equipped schools, school environments preoccupied with behavior problems, mismatches between acquired, marketable skills and career opportunities, and the resulting awareness of our increasing marginality as young adults—all contribute to the way society makes African American men invisible and undermines their interests in learning. Many young boys of African descent fight a loss of faith, feeling that the outcome of education is not worth the humiliation. (p. 94)*

The young black males I went to school with began to associate with gangs in the neighborhood during our teen years. Gang boundaries were set, and crossing the boundaries could lead to physical violence. Traveling to and from school became fraught with anxiety. The carefree childhood conversations that I had enjoyed with my peers became tainted with codes of survival. I had to learn how to respond to gang members who approached me with the question "What you ride?" (whose gang did you belong to). To avoid being jumped, some boys would lie and say they were in whatever gang they were being approached by. This could be a dangerous move. Members of one gang would sometimes pretend to be in another just to trick the boy being approached, then attack him if he gave the wrong answer. This put some boys in constant fear.

Some "gang-bangers" would carry golf clubs as instruments of torture. (There were no golf courses in our neighborhood, and Tiger Woods was ten years off.) Not much later, it seemed as though all of the young men in the neighborhood had easy access to handguns. I was made aware of the increase of guns in the neighborhood in very frightening ways. I witnessed a murder for the first time in seventh grade. In eighth grade, I saw a friend I played basketball with shot and killed. By the time I reached the ninth grade, crime was on the rise in the Chicago housing projects where I lived because of the influx of crack cocaine. I stared down the barrel of a gun three times before I was sixteen. I was caught up in a violent campaign of poor, black males pitted against other poor, black males.

Beyond what I witnessed, I was subjected to illegal searches by police officers on at least four different occasions. The only explanation for the searches is that I was a black male living in a certain neighborhood. I have been placed in a jail cell, wrongly accused, twice. The first time, I was picked up as I stood at a bus stop with a classmate. The police told us that two black males had snatched a purse from a woman at the mall. We were taken to the police station, where we were forced to wait until the victim arrived to make an ID. As I was handcuffed and placed in the back of the police car, I felt humiliated and embarrassed. For many years after that, my greatest fear was going to jail. I believed others perceived me to be a criminal, although I had never committed a crime and never intended to commit a crime.

Experiences such as these can lead to feelings of guilt and anger. I felt as if I was doing something wrong whenever I was with a group of black male peers. I would keep my hands in my pockets when shopping to avoid being viewed as a thief. Many days I would wake up longing to change my existence, but I knew that once I got up I would have to face the same stale reality. I began to identify my race as the main obstacle to my safety and upward social mobility. I became hostile toward a world I decided did not care about my existence, and I harbored that hostility for more than fifteen years. In the words of James Baldwin (1963), many black males are never able to shake their dungeons, "becoming defeated long before they die."

I found a way to cope. I learned to "park" ghetto life—to go to school without letting it infect my hopes and dreams. But my experiences extracted a psychological toll. I wondered why I had to wait ten years or maybe even a lifetime to have what I believed others outside of my community already possessed, even took for granted. Fortunately for me, reading became my saving grace. My growing interest in reading was supported both at home and in school. As a "hopeful adolescent"—a term used by Milbrey McLaughlin, Merita Irby, and Juliet Langman (1994) to refer to a youth who has effective support systems in at least one institution, such as family, a church, a community organization, specific youth-focused organizations, sports, or in some cases school—I managed to avoid becoming a "nowhere kid" (Herbert 2001). As a result, I believe in the promising possibilities associated with reading. At the same time, however, I agree with William Brozo (2002):

> To presume that reading itself will transform conditions that plague young men such as poverty, alcohol and drug abuse, crime, and irresponsible fathering is recklessly naïve; however, to ignore the potential of active literacy for ensuring that fewer adolescent males become nowhere kids is equally naïve. (p. 156)

BOYS AND READING

Several books on the topic of boys and reading have been published in the past few years, including *Masculinity Goes to School* (Gilbert and Gilbert 1998); *Misreading Masculinity: Boys, Literacy, and Popular Culture* (Newkirk 2002); *Boys, Literacies and Schooling* (Rowan, Knobel, Bigum, and Lankshear 2002); *Boys and Literacy: Exploring the Issues* (Maynard 2002); *To Be a Boy, to Be a Reader: Engaging Teen and Preteen Boys in Active Literacy* (Brozo 2002); and *Reading Don't Fix No Chevys: Literacy in the Lives of Young Men* (Smith and Wilhelm 2002). The attention to boys and their reading was stimulated by test data indicating that boys perform less well in reading compared to girls. These data, however, do not explain why boys tend to feel alienated from literacy experiences. Although all the authors of the books just cited believe that schools are attempting to address the literacy needs of boys within the classroom, as Gilbert and Gilbert (1998) note, "the ways in which these needs have been addressed have often been ineffective because they have not taken sufficient amount of the gendered construction of the boys they work with" (p. 200).

Books on reading focus on acknowledging boys' masculine identities during reading instruction. Brozo (2002), for example, suggested using literature with traditional male archetypes as an entry point into literacy for boys. Other authors have recommended making the reading curriculum more appealing to boys, who may view reading as a passive, "female" activity. Trisha Maynard (2002) suggested that boys may reject reading as a way of separating themselves from all that is female and establishing themselves as male. "If the masculine self is oppositional to the literate self," write Gilbert and Gilbert (1998), "then it must seem to many boys that literacy is relatively unimportant and irrelevant" (p. 215). In short, teachers can benefit by becoming "gender aware" in their teaching practices (Maynard 2002).

These two ideas—gender awareness and an emphasis on masculinity—have led to several specific suggestions on how to get boys involved with reading, including the following:

- Use male-oriented texts with male characters (as opposed to more female-oriented texts).
- Use texts that are apt to engage boys emotionally with the characters, that deal with issues boys care about, and that honor their identity.
- Expose boys to nonfiction that involves learning something new.
- Use texts that legitimize the male experience and support boys' view of themselves.

Michael Smith and Jeffrey Wilhelm (2002) found that although the boys they studied believed in the importance of school literacy in theory, they often rejected and resisted it in actual practice because it was not related to their immediate interests and needs. The boys wanted to get information about real events and situations. They also liked text that could be easily exported into conversations and text that provided multiple perspectives. All of the young men with whom Smith and Wilhelm worked were passionate about activities in which they experienced "flow" (Csikszentmihalyi 1990). Four conditions make up the flow experience:

1. There is a feeling of control.
2. The activities provide an appropriate level of challenge.
3. Clear goals and feedback are included.
4. The focus is on the immediate.

Unfortunately, most of the young men did not experience flow in their literature activities, at least not those in school. Therefore, the boys critiqued schooling as being superficial.

Although gender is central to the ongoing discussion about boys and reading, some have argued that boys' failure in reading is more connected to their economic station (Epstein, Elwood, Hey, and Maw 1998). Focusing on gender alone can blind us to the importance of race, class, ethnicity, and other dimensions of human experience. As Gilbert and Gilbert (1998) wrote,

> *The intersections between socio-economic resources, geographical location, ethnicity, and "race" are critical here, as they demonstrate the groups of boys who are potentially more at risk of school failure. This is particularly noticeable in literacy results, where, although gender remains a key predictor of success, it is clearly affected by a range of other social and cultural factors. (p. 9)*

However, as Maynard (2002) has pointed out, the impact of social class and race may have been understated in recent analyses of educational attainment.

SOCIOECONOMIC STATUS, RACE, AND READING

Data from the National Assessment of Educational Progress (NAEP) indicate a correlation between low levels of reading achievement and socioeconomic status. Poor students at grades 4, 8, and 12 are underperforming in reading when compared to students who are not poor. This is particularly salient when black males are considered. The reading achievement gaps are wider among adolescents. Many black male high school graduates are reading at the same level as white middle school students or below. Many of these black students attend low-achieving schools staffed with underqualified teachers who are unable to address their students' literacy needs. Also, many of these students' teachers have low expectations about their students' ability to meet high academic standards.

In *We Real Cool*, bell hooks (2004) asserts that "black males without class privilege have always been targeted for miseducation" (p. 34). Unlike poor students from other ethnic groups, such as Asians and whites, who outperform poor black males on reading assessments, black males are perceived as being intellectually inferior and incapable of handling cognitively challenging material. In short, the "problems" that black and working-class boys have with literacy at school may be linked with teachers' perceptions of the intersection between ethnicity, poverty, and schooling (Gilbert and Gilbert 1998).

Positive images of black male readers are hard to find, whether one looks in books, on television, or in professional research. This may affect the way black males view their relationship to reading. It also may affect the way teachers and society view the relationship between black boys and reading. After she wrote *Be Boy Buzz* to represent young black males and place them at the center of universal stories, bell hooks met with the illustrator who had been hired for the book. The first illustrations that were shown to her were of black boys in motion, running, jumping, and playing. She requested images of black boys being still, enjoying solitude, reading. She believed that "the image of a boy reading was particularly important to include because it is clear that this society sends black male children the message that they do not need to be readers" (2004, p. 40).

Unlike the past, noted hooks, when many black males viewed education and reading as a means to liberation, "most black boys from underprivileged classes are socialized via mass media and class-based education to believe that all that is required for their survival is the ability to do physical labor" (p. 34). Many of them do not believe that reading for intellectual development matters. These feelings of anti-intellectualism work against them. Nevertheless, anti-intellectualism is often reinforced in schools. Ellis Cose, author of *The Envy of the World: On Being a Black Man in America,* recalls that the longer he went to school the more he was convinced that real learning would not take place. Cose is not alone in feeling this way. Many young black males conclude that their teachers do not care about their literacy or their lives.

LITERACY DEVELOPMENT AND BLACK MALES

The conventional understanding is that school prepares young people for the future. So often they are told, "Stay in school and get your education." However, urban youth in particular are apt to hear this message from individuals who have not taken advantage of their own education. My mother, who earned a GED, always encouraged my brothers and me to stay in school. For black males growing up in environments where many adult males have been defaulted by school intentionally or unintentionally, the value of school to one's future is seen as a false promise. They may resist the idea that schooling has value, particularly if literacy instruction fails to be responsive to their needs. According to Smith and Wilhelm (2002), black males may reject literacy because of its future orientation, its separation from immediate uses and functions, and its emphasis on knowledge that is not valued in their life outside of school.

Many poor black males are too preoccupied with thoughts of their own mortality and the day-to-day energy required to survive to think about literacy as a bridge to the future. You can hear it in their music. You can hear it in their writing. You can hear the preoccupation with death in their conversations. Alex Kotlowitz chronicles the lives of two young black boys, Lafeyette and Pharoah, over a span of two years in his book *There Are No Children Here* (1991). Here are some examples of how they and their friends felt as they tried to survive in a Chicago housing project, just around the time I was graduating from a high school not many miles away.

> "We're going to die one way or the other," says one boy, "by killing or plain out, I just want to die plain out" (p. 51).

> Eighteen-year-old Craig, wrote Kotlowitz, "had thought about his future, something most of the young men in this neighborhood rejected—often for a good reason—as a waste of time" (p. 121).

> Pharoah, age ten, "had begun to resign himself to the possibility that he might die young" (p. 154).

> When Craig died, Lafeyette was shattered. He started thinking, "I ain't doing nothing, I could get killed, or if not get killed I might go to jail for something I didn't do." (His brother, another black male, was wrongly convicted of robbery.) "I could die any minute," Lafeyette figured, "so I ain't going to be scared of nothing" (pp. 208–209).

> According to Kotlowitz, neither Ricky, age thirteen, nor Lafeyette "knew what he wanted to be when he grew up. That seemed too far away. They spent so much energy just thinking about the present, how could they be expected to think about the future?" (p. 221).

> Pharoah, now eleven, told a friend, "I worry about dying, dying at an early age, while you're little. I'll be thinking about it I want to get out of the jects [Chicago housing projects]. I want to get out. It ain't no joke when you die" (p. 264).

Lafayette and Pharoah's mother described her neighborhood to Kotlowitz as "not a neighborhood that allows adolescents room for mistakes" (p. 301).

Literacy instruction must have value in these young people's current time and space if it is to attract and sustain their attention. It must address their issues and concerns in a way that will lead them to examine their own lives. Although addressing the literacy needs of young black males may not be enough to curb the social ills that plague such young people, it is something teachers can do that will surely help.

Although many books have been written about the relationship between boys and reading, and others have been written about African American youth culture and urban youth (Mahiri 1998; Mahiri 2004), as well as African American males in school and society (Kunjufu 1995; Polite and Davis 1999), I have chosen to focus specifically on reading among black males, particularly those who are learning to read amid turmoil, for several reasons. First, increased reading achievement and literacy development among America's poor black males can provide them with greater opportunity to participate in all the good that America has to offer. It can also lead to higher levels of college enrollment, lower levels of unemployment, a reduction in violent crime, and lower incarceration rates for black men. These issues are never mentioned in the books on reading that do not focus specifically on black males. And the books on black males do not focus on reading or offer specific instructional approaches teachers can use with their black male students. Second, as mentioned earlier, black males are increasingly skeptical that education can help them escape from their low economic strata. Many of these young men believe that their fate has been determined and that failure is inevitable. The turmoil in their lives is so intense they are unable to see beyond it, and they do not believe anyone cares about them. They do not embrace the idea that text can transform their world, because there are too few examples in their neighborhoods to suggest this can be true. Third, the image of the troubled black male reader permeates the subconscious of many teachers in America's classrooms, though in many cases, the reading failures of these young men are exacerbated by poor-quality instruction.

Curricula and educational plans have fallen short of addressing the academic, cultural, emotional, and social needs of black males. They need better literacy teaching. Many of these young men are seeking a balance between taking their minds off the pain associated with poverty and sustaining hope for the future. Poverty has a way of souring the child-hood of many black males. I believe that reading has a way of sweetening it.

This book provides a different perspective than other books on boys and reading. For one thing, it is more reflective in nature. I myself was a black boy who learned to read amid turmoil. Eventually I began teaching other black males who were learning to read amid turmoil. Now I provide professional development for teachers of black males who are learning to read amid turmoil. These three lenses have guided my writing. My aim is to help educators reconceptualize the role of literacy for their black male students to ensure that they are offered the best literacy instruction possi-ble. In the following pages I describe the critical factors that affect black male literacy, black males' response to these factors, and the teachers' role in managing them. I offer a framework for addressing the literacy needs of these students. I hope to provide a pathway toward continued progress for those committed, or those yet to become committed, to the struggle to ensure that poor black males are offered the literacy opportunities that all of America's children deserve.

CHAPTER 2

TURMOIL AND THE PROMISE OF READING

And he fell against the tree, sinking to the ground and clutching the roots of the tree. He shouted in silence and only silence answered—and yet, when he cried, his cry had caused a ringing in the outermost limits of the earth. This ringing, his lone cry rolling through creation, frightening the sleeping fish and fowl, awakening echoes everywhere, river, and valley, and mountain wall, caused in him a fear so great that he lay for a moment silent and trembling at the base of the tree, as though he wished to be buried there. But that burdened heart of his would not be still, would not let him keep silence—would not let him breathe until he cried again. And so he cried again; and his cry returned again; and still the silence waited for God to speak.

James Baldwin, *Go Tell It on the Mountain*

n *Go Tell It on the Mountain,* his first novel, James Baldwin describes the repeated cry of a young black man named Gabriel. Today the wails of real-life black males can still be heard, as they struggle to survive in communities of turmoil. I was reminded of this turmoil a while ago when I read a newspaper headline describing an event in the Chicago neighborhood I grew up in, which was recently described as a "second America" in the book *Our America: Life and Death on the South Side of Chicago* (Jones, Newman, and Isay 1998). The neighborhood has limited resources and few glimmers of hope for those who are trapped in its awful narrative. In 1994, my old neighborhood was the backdrop of a murder that made national headlines. Two boys were found guilty of throwing a five-year-old boy from the window of an abandoned fourteenth-floor apartment in a high-rise building. The five-year-old was killed because he had refused to steal candy from a nearby grocery store. The child murderers attended my former elementary school.

Recently, I returned to the apartment building where I was raised to see what had become of the neighborhood. The block where I lived had become an eyesore. Three sets of initials spray-painted on the outside of the building over twenty years earlier had never been removed. Five of the six apartments in my old building were vacant, their windows covered with thick slabs of wood. The hall was dark, and the metal mailboxes that had been attached to the wall had been removed. A large green dumpster filled with garbage was sitting on its side near the curb.

When I was a teenager, I felt ashamed of where I lived. This shame led me to the most painful decision I ever made. At fourteen, I chose to leave my mother and go live with my father, who was at that time living in a middle-class neighborhood. The pain on my mother's face is as clear to me now as it was the night I left. Yet I found comfort leaving my mother because living in the ghetto had made me feel as though I lived outside of America, on the periphery of prosperity, against a glass shield that allowed me to peep in but not participate. I needed to escape. The stay with my father, however, was short-lived. I eventually was forced to return home.

When I was a boy, Saturday nights were the times I feared the most. That was the time my parents would occasionally go out to party, returning between 1:00 and 3:00 a.m. Then their fighting would start. Awakened by their angry voices, I would get up and beg them to stop. My father would shout, "Go back to bed!"—as if this would insulate me from the sounds of my mother's frantic screams. My brother and I could only wait for the fighting to end and hope that Mom was not hurt too badly.

One night she managed to overpower my father. She grabbed a wide-blade butcher's knife from the kitchen and stabbed him within a few inches of his heart. Several neighbors who came to see what was happening pleaded with her to call an ambulance. She lit a cigarette, turned the music on, and said, "Let him die." She dragged him into the hallway of our three-story brown brick walkup and slammed the door. I was terrified, certain that this was the night I would become a fatherless son with an imprisoned mother.

The general turmoil engendered by poverty and the domestic violence in my family could have had a negative effect on my literacy development. Turmoil, however, does not automatically lead to stunted literacy. Many black males who come from violent homes and troubled communities manage to achieve high levels of literacy. Responsive and meaningful literacy instruction can nurture the resiliency of black males and can encourage them to value the written word.

As a child, I would sit on my bed reading for hours, trying to imagine what it would be like to be Laura Ingalls and live on the prairie. I would also read Nancy Drew and Hardy Boys books and get scared all by myself, engrossed in their mysterious journeys. I would cheer as they figured out the mysteries, especially when my predictions were correct. I could even feel the pain of the overweight and self-conscious white girl in *The Cat Ate My Gym Suit,* who was ridiculed in her gym class, telling the teacher the cat ate her gym suit. I loved to read, although my home and my neighborhood were far from perfect. Reading ignited my childhood curiosity.

Reading would also lead me to personal discoveries. During the last few years of my parents' strained marriage, I discovered that I could have a personal conversation with God. I always knew that I could holler out his name and pray for the violence to stop. I also knew that I could pray for a new Huffy bicycle on Christmas morning. But these were special circumstances. I did not discover that I could just talk to him or write to him until I met Margaret, a young adolescent girl suffering through puberty, in *Are You There, God? It's Me, Margaret.* Judy Blume, the author who introduced me to Margaret, became my favorite writer.

Through reading I also became aware of my differences. In his preface to *Invisible Man,* Ralph Ellison explains how odd, unexpected things give shape and form to our lives. We are shaped by both major and minor events. A major event that shaped my own life was *Roots,* a television miniseries based on a novel written by Alex Haley. This on-screen history lesson introduced me to the Middle Passage and its horrors. Viewing whippings and violations of black bodies by slave masters filled me with hatred. I no longer felt compassion for all people. My most lasting impression was of Kunta Kinte being whipped into "Tobyhood." Observing the mistreatment of blacks in *Roots* was a life-changing experience for me. Though not consciously aware of it at the time, I began to look upon the world with a new set of filters—filters that also influenced the way I read print.

In fifth grade, I began to read the junior detective series Encyclopedia Brown. As I read the various entries in the series, insidious thoughts began to intrude. I did not have a tree house. I had never gone to a garage sale because there were no garages in my neighborhood. There were no lemonade stands run by children. I realized that Encyclopedia Brown lived in a different world from me. This character's world was free of suffocative elements rooted in historical mistreatment.

It was around the same time in my life that I read about an anxious young Jewish boy preparing for his bar mitzvah. I concluded that something was missing in my life. What was *my* rite of passage? How would I determine when I was entering a new phase in my life? Was my rite of passage my first French kiss at the age of eleven? Was it the time I had what I thought was a real sexual experience at the age of twelve? As I compared my life with those of characters in the books I was reading, I came to feel as though my development was being charted in insignificant waters.

I started to believe that there was a white world and a black world, and that I lived in the black one. This idea became reinforced after a teacher introduced our class to the poetry of Langston Hughes, Paul Laurence Dunbar, Claude McKay, Countee Cullen, and Amiri Baraka. One particular poem, by Countee Cullen, stands out in my mind. It describes a black boy who went to Baltimore. The boy experienced many things there, but what stood out in his mind was the time a white boy, who was not much bigger than he, faced him and called him nigger. This poem angered me.

In search of my own rites of passage and knowledge of my black self, I began to search for books more closely aligned with my own life. This search was launched during a library visit one day when I ventured into the adult section. A novel on the revolving book holder leaped out at me— Dick Gregory's autobiographical novel *Nigger*. Printed on the book jacket, near the penetrating hue of the author's complexion, were the words "over a million copies sold." I was eleven years old and had never purchased a book.

I decided to take a trip to a bookstore and buy a copy of *Nigger*. Entering a bookstore for the first time, I was flabbergasted. It was huge. There were so many books. I had no idea how they were organized, so I approached the information desk for help. A woman escorted me down an aisle and told me that the books were arranged in alphabetical order by authors' last names. She directed me to the *G*s. I was amazed that there were so many other books in the section I found myself in—the Afro-American literature section of the store.

The bus ride home would take thirty minutes, so I decided to start reading my new book. I was absorbed by Gregory's poignant depiction of his struggle as a young impoverished black boy. He spoke to my experiences. I connected. Reading the book released my childhood dreams from the constraints of ghetto poverty. The hope in Dick Gregory's book ignited something in me. Despite his absent, drunken father, the rags he wore to school, and the insults he received because of his dark complexion, the main character never let his dreams die.

Although I had been introduced to a few black authors in school by teachers who read excerpts of their works, I did not understand why we were not reading more of this "black stuff"—books by black authors. Some of my classmates had no idea that there were so many books written by black authors who shared our experiences and provided answers to some of our problems. I don't think I would have discovered them when I did if it were not for that trip to the bookstore.

After reading *Nigger,* I wanted to find strength through reading about the struggles of other blacks in literature. This led me to Richard Wright's *Black Boy* and Booker T. Washington's *Up from Slavery.* I was hooked by both authors. William Brozo (2002) would say that I discovered "male archetypes" on which to base my life. Even as I continued to read books on other subjects, I began to seek out writings about the black experience in the United States. I became more inclined to read literature that helped me understand America's perception of who I was and what I was expected to become. I began to change my self-definition; I embraced my blackness. As a child, I resented my brothers' referring to me as "darker than me"—being darker than they were. As I learned about the historical mistreatment of blacks and the indoctrination of inferiority based on skin color, I could understand my family's misguided notions of blackness. "Darker than me" became my private badge of authenticity because of the literature that I read.

Although I did not fully understand all of the authors' works on first reading them, I was able to understand their basic messages. Langston Hughes taught me that "Life Ain't No Crystal Stair." Booker T. Washington showed me how to come up from slavery. Richard Wright taught me how to resist a community that does not believe in a black boy's dream. The power of the language tucked away in these authors' books became my road map, my game plan to sidestep the turmoil I experienced.

Several junior high school teachers also helped me avoid becoming swallowed up by the turmoil that surrounded me. They helped me understand more about texts and more about the world. I recall my sixth-grade teacher defining the word *inalienable* as she read the Declaration of Independence. That year I was also introduced to the words *altruistic, indefatigable, tranquility, reciprocity, tenacious, dilapidated,* and *chaos.* My sixth-grade teacher, a short woman, was a giant among giants, a builder of large dreams. My seventh- and eighth-grade teachers helped make the dreams real. While other teachers in my school were planning enough assignments to keep kids busy to get through the day, these teachers stood before me as passports to the future. They helped me study Dr. Martin Luther King Jr.'s "I Have a Dream" speech. When he stated that America's promissory note was marked "insufficient funds," I understood. I began to see the ambiguity of being black and American. My teachers empowered me with words that other teachers believed were for the "other" kids, not poor black boys attending a school situated just yards from a federally funded housing project where single welfare mothers lived.

While many of the students in my school were growing into the neighborhood, finding permanent lodging in the spiraling turmoil, I was able to chart a different course. Caring teachers with high expectations helped me read my way out. They helped me push against the currents of the environment in which I lived. They did not limit their aspirations for me because my pants were too short. They did not lower expectations for me because my lunch application told them I lived below the poverty line. Instead, they required me to read the basal textbook, as well as the local newspaper, historical documents, poetry, and literature. These teachers had Harvard dreams for students living in hellish conditions. I felt a kinship with them that helped me attend to their instruction. Literacy was thrust upon me in rich and meaningful ways, not because I was a wonderful student, but because the teachers believed I deserved nothing less. I was a young adolescent being apprenticed toward success. Literacy, based on concepts of culture, community, and caring, was the vehicle to that success.

Because of the teachers I had and the authors I read, my reading habits developed and my thinking patterns changed. They responded to my cry, which was not unlike Gabriel's cry in the epigraph of this chapter. I am not sure if I would have continued to read if I came to the conclusion that it was not worthwhile. I am not sure I would have continued to read if I could not see the connection between what I was reading and my own life. I am afraid to contemplate how my life would be different if my teachers had taken a functional orientation toward reading instruction, focusing, for example, on decontextualized skills and strategies, a currently popular instructional approach prompted by the widespread emphasis on raising standardized test scores. With the No Child Left Behind mandate, schools across the United States are striving to close the reading achievement gap between high-achieving and low-achieving students. Yet black male students continue to lag behind.

CHAPTER 3

BLACK MALES AND THE READING ACHIEVEMENT GAP

But seriously, because you both fail to understand what is happening to you. You cannot see or hear or smell the truth of what you see—and you, looking for destiny! It's classic! And the boy, this automaton, he was made of the very mud of the region and he sees far less than you. Poor stumblers, neither of you can see the other. To you he is a mark on the scorecard of your achievement, a thing and not a man; a child, or even less—a black amorphous thing. And you, for all your power, are not a man to him, but a God, a force.

Ralph Ellison, *Invisible Man*

The achievement gap between black students and white students was first noted over forty years ago. At that time, the gap was said to be mainly attributable to the family background of the students. Since then, other explanations—including peer groups, culture, discrimination, heredity, and schooling—have been offered. We now know more about what the causes and consequences of the achievement gap are than about how to close it. Several remedies have been tried—reducing class size, providing students with options to attend private schools through voucher programs, monitoring students' progress through high-stakes accountability systems, eliminating tracking, and implementing comprehensive reforms that focus on literacy. Each approach succeeded in narrowing the reading achievement gap between black and white students in the setting where it was applied. Still, the difference in educational attainment between black students and white students is one of the most stubborn and pernicious manifestations of racial inequality in our country (Chubb and Loveless 2002).

Four major barriers stand in the way of closing the reading achievement gap between poor black adolescent males and other students. First, no clear strategy has emerged on how to attain this goal. Second, no clear definition of the role of literacy instruction for black males exists. Third, educators disagree on how to provide effective reading instruction for struggling readers, particularly for those past the primary grades. Fourth, educators and policymakers have focused on strategy and skill instruction while ignoring curriculum orientation, forms of pedagogy, and other factors found to be effective in increasing the reading achievement of African American students. Some simply believe it is too late to help adolescents become better readers and prefer to focus their attention on students in the primary grades.

Placing statistical data at the center of literacy reform efforts is a mistake. Using statistical data to frame conversations about the academic underachievement of black males provides limited information on why the gap exists and how it can be closed. Monitoring reading data too easily can become a scorecard of achievement. This can lead teachers to select a text based on the requirements of standardized tests or limit instruction to test-preparation practice. Such an approach overlooks consideration of why some teachers are more effective than others in advancing the literacy of black males.

Effective teachers of black males understand that they must go beyond reading instruction. They understand, as my own teachers did, that focusing only on skills and strategies does little to address the turmoil many black youths experience in America, and it may do little to improve their reading achievement. My teachers understood that my life experiences and how I responded to these experiences mattered. They understood that the texts they placed before me had to address some of the psychological and emotional scarring that results from the day-to-day experiences of being black, male, and poor in America. My teachers wanted to help me develop an identity that would be useful outside the walls of my school.

I recall the time in eighth grade when I came to school with a "Chicago Curl," a processed hairdo. I remember how wonderful it felt to have thin, curly hair. As I prepared to cross the threshold of the classroom where the teacher greeted us each morning, I was asked to step aside. After the other students had entered the classroom, my teacher asked me why I changed my hair. Somehow, I knew this teacher believed I was misguided in my decision. I said nothing. She told me that she expected a response later, after I read a book that she promised to bring me the next day.

This teacher used my hairstyle as a reason to introduce me to a text. She gave me a copy of *The Autobiography of Malcolm X* and a question: Why did you do what you did? Her giving me this book was her way of getting me to examine America's definition of beauty and how black features (for example, thick, course hair) were considered ugly. Or perhaps she had noticed that I was being influenced by the street culture in hopes of becoming "one of the boys" and wanted me to think carefully about my actions.

My eighth-grade teacher understood that her role as a teacher needed to go beyond helping me do well on the Reading Mastery Program that our school district was then using to measure reading achievement. She was concerned about my identity. She understood something about the turmoil Malcolm X had experienced in his life, and saw a connection between his text and my life. Somehow, she knew that, in order to teach me, she had to move beyond the mandated reading curriculum that was in fact specifically designed to increase my reading achievement. She understood that focusing on reading skills and strategies to yield better reading results is insufficient when other awareness needs to be developed.

Addressing the literacy needs of poor black males requires that teachers integrate knowledge from several fields—education, sociology, anthropology, and social work, to name just some—in their instruction. Doing so is their best chance to avoid instructional practices that inadvertently contribute to the turmoil—instructional approaches that black males may resist. To move beyond what I have referred to as a mistake or functional detour, teachers and administrators must include, *but not be limited by,* research-based reading practices. In addition, several other factors need to be considered when planning effective literacy instruction for black males, because these factors have the potential to interrupt literacy development:

1. The roots of black male turmoil.
2. The black male's response to turmoil.
3. The ways institutions have responded to this turmoil.
4. How this turmoil affects black males' literacy development.

ROOTS OF BLACK MALE TURMOIL

The turmoil that black males experience is deeply rooted in the history of America. Joseph White and James Cones (1999), in their book *Black Man Emerging,* assert that the story of black men in America has three beginnings. The first has to do with their past in Africa; the second, the coming of the slave ship; and the third is the period after the Civil War.

The socialization of boys in West Africa, the hub of the slave trade, carefully follows a series of steps designed to prepare young men for their adult male roles and responsibilities. In this first beginning in Africa, White and Cones explain, boys were gradually able to develop a sense of personal power and shared values—qualities essential to attain an adequate definition of self, identity, and masculinity. Historically, the African male did not have to justify his existence as a human being, nor was he forced to deal with race as a barrier to self-worth.

In what White and Cones identify as the second beginning, African males experienced psychological and spiritual shock as they were shipped from Africa in chains and forced into slavery in America. Once they found themselves in America, these uprooted African men experienced two significant changes:

1. As slaves, they would have no legal rights or political power.
2. They would be forced to live according to a Euro-American worldview, which differed dramatically from the one that had shaped their lives.

Although the enslaved black male resisted the psychological effects of slavery, expressed self-determination, and created a culture of his own, after years of conditioning he eventually came to believe he was an inferior being.

Black male inferiority was reinforced in White and Cones' third beginning—the post-Civil War period—through racial "science" (such as the eugenics movement), legislation, and the arts. These features of American society cemented black males into a subservient role. Stereotypes of the black male became part of America's national character. The image of the black male as a subhuman, unintelligent, sexually promiscuous, idle buffoon was everywhere—in stage shows, novels, advertisements, newspapers, and magazines—and it took hold of the American psyche. Social barriers were set up to keep black men in a subordinate role. Any attempt they made to do away with these images was met with violence (including lynching) and Jim Crow laws. These barriers, along with educational, economic, political, and social disenfranchisement, made it nearly impossible for black males *as a group* to climb above the bottom rung of the social ladder in jobs, education, income, and political power.

This is the historical context that contributes to black male turmoil. But there are, in addition, several present-day factors that exacerbate the turmoil black males experience in today's society (Kitwana 2002):

1. The effect of globalization.
2. Urban economic neglect.
3. Mass media and popular culture.
4. Public policy regarding criminal justice.
5. The persistence of racial discrimination.
6. The crumbling black community infrastructure.
7. The lack of fulfillment of civil rights promises.

Today's black males are growing up in an era of globalization that has adversely affected their communities by contributing to urban economic neglect as job opportunities have become scarce for them and their families. Many urban communities are populated with low-skilled workers who have little opportunity for job growth. The unemployment rates of black youth have risen while multinational companies have grown larger. The result has been an overall decline in the quality of life for young blacks during the 1980s and 1990s, which has ushered in higher levels of drug-related crime and violence.

An economic downturn and the realization among many young blacks that the anticipated promises of the civil rights era have not materialized have caused them to believe that the American dream and the prosperity reflected in the media are unattainable for them. Other media images—those projected in black gangster films from the 1980s and '90s—*Juice, Menace II Society, New Jack City,* and *Belly*—have had a twofold effect. First, by presenting black males as out of control and dangerous, and by making black maleness synonymous with drugs and violence, these forms of popular culture created a fear of black males that ratcheted up America's war on drugs. The resulting criminal justice legislation and practices (such as mandatory minimum sentences and more vigilant policing of neighborhoods) dramatically increased the black male prison population, eventually making prison culture part of black male culture. Second, given the prevalence of negative images in the mass media and the lack of more positive representations in the media and other institutions, many black males have adopted and continue to adopt images of criminality as their identity. Few developments have altered black life as much as the incarceration of young blacks and the influence of prison on black youth culture (Kitwana 2002). These changes, along with continuing racial discrimination, have contributed to the turmoil experienced by today's generation of young black males.

The history of black males and their present condition in America are generally overlooked when educators plan literacy reforms for this group. This lack of attention has been dubbed "racial amnesia" (Dyson 2001). The failure of institutions to acknowledge or adequately respond to the needs of black males, instead blaming these youths for what is really the institutions' own failure, has caused black youths to respond to turmoil in their own way.

BLACK MALE RESPONSE TO TURMOIL

Of course, black males are not a monolithic group. Their responses to turmoil are influenced by the intensity of the turmoil they experience and the resources they have to help them cope. They react in ways that they believe will best shield them from the type and intensity of turmoil they experience. In fact, many black males are resilient; they manage to "survive the gauntlet," as Richard Majors and Jacob Gordon put it (1993). This resiliency is reflected in two fairly recent books, *The Pact* (Davis, Jenkins, Hunt, and Page 2002) and *A Hope in the Unseen* (Suskind 1999), which describe the academic journeys of four black males. But black youths' responses to the turmoil in their lives can also be connected to academic underperformance.

Although black males have developed multiple survival techniques throughout their history in the United States, the "cool pose" is perhaps unique. This pose, a ritualized form of masculinity, uses certain behavior, scripts, physical posturing, and carefully crafted performance to convey a strong impression of pride, strength, and control. The cool pose is a coping mechanism to hide self-doubt, insecurity, and inner turmoil, and can be observed in such things as dress (for example, beltless pants hanging below the waist), manner of talk (signifying, rapping), and behavior (high fives, special handshakes, forms of greeting). The black male adopts the cool pose as a way to:

- Cope with oppression, invisibility, and marginality.
- Communicate power, toughness, detachment, and style.
- Maintain a balance between his inner life and his social environment.
- Cope with conflict and anxiety.
- Render him visible and empower him.
- Neutralize stress.
- Manage his feelings of rage in the face of prejudice and discrimination.
- Counter the negative forces in his life.

Although adopting a cool pose as a coping mechanism can in some ways be positive, it can have negative consequences:

- The black male's potential and growth are thwarted because of his refusal to involve himself in experiences that could help expand his personal, social, and political consciousness.
- The black male can get into trouble with authorities who lack understanding of the use of the behavior as a coping mechanism.
- His inclination to disclose little about himself makes it difficult for teachers and others interested in his welfare to provide him with necessary support.
- His refusal to retreat in the face of violence can lead to personal harm and increased fatalities for black males generally.
- They avoid institutions and activities that are considered "uncool"—including schools, museums, churches, and other institutions that could help them alleviate their turmoil.

Two poems capture black males' use of the cool pose and the way they use masks to protect themselves. The first is "We Real Cool" by Gwendolyn Brooks, the former poet laureate of Illinois:

We real cool.
We Left school.
We Lurk late.
We Strike straight.
We Sing sin.
We Thin gin.
We Jazz June.
We Die soon.

Paul Laurence Dunbar wrote "We Wear the Mask":

We wear the mask that grins and lies,
It hides our cheeks and shades our eyes,—
This debt we pay to human guile;
With torn and bleeding hearts we smile,
And mouth with myriad subtleties,

Why should the world be over-wise,
In counting all our tears and sighs?
Nay, let them only see us, while
We wear the mask.

We smile, but, O great Christ, our cries
To thee from tortured souls arise.
We sing, but oh the clay is vile
Beneath our feet, and long the mile;
But let the world dream otherwise,
We wear the mask.

Black males also react to the turmoil in their lives with anger. This is illustrated in the gangsta rap that became so popular in the late 1980s with the emergence of the rap group NWA (Niggaz With Attitudes). The hostile lyrics of this group reflected no respect for authority and glorified violent acts and those who perform them. The members of the group expressed their anger in songs such as "F—k the Police." Their songs are filled with posturing and a lack of respect for authority that ultimately leads to incarceration.

Rap music also reflects a loss of hope and limited aspirations for the future. In one of his posthumous releases, Tupac Shakur, a slain black male rapper, states, "The promise of a better tomorrow ain't never reached me because my teachers were too petrified in class to teach me." Shakur's suggested mistrust of his school environment and confusion about his place in the world is not unique. They are feelings shared by many black males on reaching adolescence. The stress that results from this confusion leads young black men to three different kinds of response (Akbar 1992):

1. Black males' denial or rejection of their own cultural values as they attempt to assimilate in the dominant white culture.
2. Overidentification with the antiblack hostility in the dominant white American culture.
3. Acts of self-destruction that result from faulty attempts to cope with the frustration they feel as a consequence of the barriers to growth and the absence of a sense of security and well-being they face under racially oppressive conditions.

Conflict often exists between institutions and black males because those in the establishment lack understanding, or misunderstand, the cultural-specific behaviors exhibited by black males.

INSTITUTIONAL RESPONSES

Institutional responses to black male turmoil vary. Some are designed to help black males move beyond the turmoil; others are punitive in nature, their intent being to stamp out black males' responses to turmoil. Many discussions have taken place in recent years among individuals as well as public and private organizations at the local, state, and federal levels to determine how to better support black males in the communities in which they live, to come up with ways to make conditions better for them in the larger society, and generally to improve their social, economic, and educational situations.

While the needs of other groups are generally addressed by the U.S. Commission on Civil Rights, black males have recently been the focus of state and national commissions formed specifically for them. The presence of turmoil in their lives is usually acknowledged in the names and mission statements of the various commissions. For example, the Indiana Commission on African American Males was formerly called the Commission on Socially Disadvantaged Black Males. It was established to identify and recommend public remedies to increase, broaden, and improve the economic, educational, social, and professional status of black males in the state. The Initiative on Black Men and Boys in the District of Columbia was established to study the life circumstances of African American men in the United States and why their problems constitute one of the most formidable domestic challenges facing our country today.

As mentioned earlier, however, other responses to black male turmoil have been punitive in nature. Over the past twenty years the United States has invested more in prisons than education. According to the study *Cellblocks or Classrooms? The Funding of Higher Education and Corrections and Its Impact on African American Men* (Justice Policy Institute 2002), spending on corrections grew at six times the rate of state spending on higher education between 1980 and 2000. During this same time period, the total number of prison inmates in the United States grew from 500,000 to over 2 million. African Americans make up roughly half of the total, although they are only around 13 percent of the U.S. population. The increased investment in prisons was made as a result of the war on drugs and its associated violence. What this essentially meant was that young, black male drug dealers were targeted. Young black men had turned in droves to dealing drugs in the 1980s in an attempt to escape poverty. The lack of job opportunities coupled with the influx of drugs in many urban communities led to the temptation of quick money for many black males.

Schools have responded both positively and negatively to black male turmoil. To remedy black males' underachievement, some educators established schools and community programs specifically to educate black males—for example, Detroit's Malcolm X Academy (Watson and Smitherman 1996). The pioneering work of Dr. Clifford Watson led to the creation of two African American immersion schools in Milwaukee. It also led to the creation of the Ujamaa Institute in New York with an African-centered curriculum and African-centered "rites of passage" programs for males that were also adopted in other places, such as Baltimore, Cleveland, San Diego, and North Carolina. Establishing these schools and programs was believed to be necessary in order to counter the poor performance of black males in more typical school settings. The difficulties traditional schools inadvertently create for black males in turmoil are many. Here are just a few:

- Micro-aggression—that is, the minor things teachers do or say on a day-to-day basis that can anger their black male students. This includes statements by the teacher such as "I am not going to let you play basketball if you don't do your work" or "If you practiced your math as much as you practiced your rappin' you wouldn't be failing." With statements like these, teachers unconsciously project stereotypical images of black males (Pierce 1970).

- Psychometric warfare. Often, so-called scientific data (for example, test or IQ scores) are used to support the notion of differential learning capacities between whites and blacks. Teachers use test data to reduce the difficult problems black students face into intellectually simplistic descriptions. This allows the teachers to ignore the historical truths and the cultural principles of their African American students. Testing can become the ultimate approach for defining black students' abilities (Nobles 1987).

- Misguided educational placements. Educators sometimes choose to place black males in special classes rather than develop culturally appropriate practices to help in their education. For example, black males are often found in lower academic tracks, although the practice of tracking has not yielded positive results. In fact, tracking actually results in the undereducation of many black males. They become handicapped, victims of the school. Only rarely are black male students found in programs for the gifted.

- Barriers to learning. Poor black young people, male and female, often must attend schools characterized by poorly prepared teachers, inadequate educational facilities, low teacher expectations, and ineffective administrators.

- Expulsion and suspension. The expulsion and suspension rates of black males are disproportionately higher than all other groups. In some cases, these rates are excessive. For example, in one school district, black males make up 12 percent of the student population but almost 40 percent of all suspensions. And this district is far from being unique.

In short, schools are hostile and unpredictable environments for many black males, who come to view themselves as nonachievers and nonparticipants in society because of what happens to them there. Many of these young men begin to feel like victims—victims of race and poverty. These perceptions, whether real or imagined, have an impact on their reading achievement.

ADDRESSING MULTIPLE LITERACIES

Ideally, young black men living amid turmoil would value print and understand that literacy has the power to improve their educational, social, and economic situations. In reality, however, it can be hard for boys who witness acts of violence or have friends or relatives who fall victim to violence to see long-term investment in school as anything other than trivial. It is important for teachers to at least be aware of the impact of turmoil on their black male students' literacy development. Without this understanding, there is the potential for conflict between teachers and their black male students, particularly among teachers who misunderstand certain cultural-specific behaviors (for example, young men's assuming a cool pose or avoiding self-disclosure).

Teachers can misinterpret black males' attempt to "wear the mask" as indolence or lack of concern for their future. Misinterpretations of black males' behavior or misinterpretation of their reaction to the turmoil in their life can be exacerbated by ineffective teaching strategies and a teacher's negative views of black males and their learning potential. This can lead to a kind of negative reciprocity. On one hand, the student thinks the teacher does not care whether he learns, so he is less apt to make an effort. On the other, the teacher thinks that the student does not care about his learning so she puts forth minimal effort to teach him. This is a catch-22 that leads to mutual mistrust and, in turn, to academic underperformance by the black male student.

Unless teachers adjust their instruction and seek professional development that takes into account some of the things described in this chapter, the trend of poor literacy development in traditional school settings among poor black males will continue. It is highly likely that these young people will continue to retreat from instruction, mistrust teachers and schools, be brought down by the idea that the future is dismal, and be penalized for the mechanisms they use to protect their identity and their masculinity. As long as the focus is on increasing test scores—something that is irrelevant to many of these young men—to the exclusion of the more significant factors described throughout this chapter, black males will continue to struggle. Literacy instruction must be planned with a complete understanding of the turmoil experienced by black males. The presence of turmoil in the lives of black male students, their reaction to it, and institutional reactions have implications for pedagogical practices, classroom interactions, and curriculum orientations. Literacy instruction must be planned in ways to advance multiple literacies in the lives of black males. Figure 3.1 displays the multiple literacies that teachers should foster:

■ Academic literacy—skills and strategies that can be applied independently to handle cognitively demanding tasks.

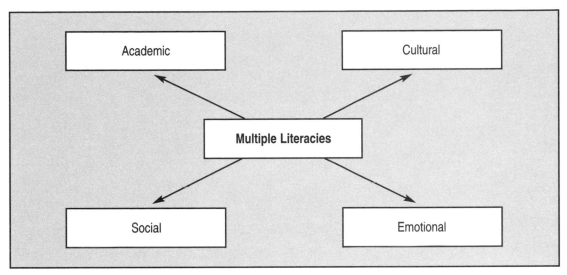

FIGURE 3.1 Multiple Literacies

- Cultural literacy—a consciousness of historical and current events that shapes one's cultural identity as an African American; knowledge of the rich and storied history of African Americans and what this means in present-day situations; a sense of one's cultural identity.
- Emotional literacy—the ability to manage one's feelings and beliefs.
- Social literacy—the ability to navigate a variety of settings with people with similar or dissimilar views; being able to communicate in a variety of ways to achieve positive outcomes.

Teachers must become personally invested in their black male students in a way that moves beyond the existing curriculum. Instruction must take place in responsive environments where the literacies of black males can flourish. This is the focus of the next chapters.

RECONCEPTUALIZING THE ROLE OF LITERACY INSTRUCTION

Bewildered we are passion-tossed, mad with the madness of a mobbed and mocked and murdered people; straining at the armposts of Thy throne, we raise our shackled hand and charge Thee, God, by the bones of our stolen fathers, by the tears or our dead mothers, by the very blood of Thy crucified Christ: What meaneth this? Tell us the plan; give us the sign!

W. E. B. Du Bois, *Darkwater: Voices Within the Veil*

n this chapter, I offer a framework for advancing the literacy of black males. This framework consists of various facets, or "strands," for theory, instruction, and professional development, and is based on my experiences as a middle school teacher, my research with struggling African American adolescent readers and their teachers, and practices educators have found to be successful with students of color. Though the instructional strands are often of most interest to teachers, principals, and district administrators in their effort to improve the reading achievement of black male students who are not performing well in schools, it would be a mistake to focus solely on instructional details. Teachers must also give attention to more general issues—the role of literacy instruction in the lives of black males, forms of pedagogy that have been effective, and appropriate curriculum planning and text selection. Teachers also can benefit from professional development and ongoing inquiry into literacy practices that can benefit their students. For these reasons I include theoretical and professional-development strands in the overall framework outlined in this chapter, to help teachers move beyond the limitations of the instructional strands.

The overall goal of this framework is to help teachers and administrators create classrooms where black males receive literacy instruction that both promotes academic excellence and nurtures a positive identity of who they are and what they can become—classrooms that are nesting grounds for literacy development. Having the classroom be a nurturing environment is essential because too many black males see schools and classrooms as unwelcoming, hostile environments. One experience in particular convinced me that this is the case.

Over the course of four months, I invited a black male in his mid-thirties who was recently released from prison to join me for weekly trips to a bookstore. I introduced him to provocative texts and had several lengthy conversations with him about them. I started with books about the black male experience in America, such as *Makes Me Wanna Holler: A Young Black Man in America* (McCall 1995). Within weeks, our readings and discussions had moved beyond the "cultural hooks" I had used to texts that I thought would help him examine his present economic condition. To this end, I selected *The End of Work* (Rifkin 1995) and *The Good Society* (Galbraith 1996). The Rifkin book discusses the displacement of low-skill labor by technology; the Galbraith book describes how society cannot function without low-skill labor. After my companion had read these two books, we discussed the impact these issues had on his economic advancement.

By the time we were nearing the end of our meetings at the bookstore, I was frustrated. I couldn't see how reading and discussion would solve this man's problem of finding employment. I began to doubt the utility of reading as a means to empowerment without other forms of support that would address the most urgent needs of people like him. During our last trip to the bookstore I shared my doubts with my companion. He lifted my spirits when he said, "Man, this is the nesting ground." I asked him what he meant and he added, "This is the nourishment that feeds the mind." This man was holding on to his belief in the power of the written word when I was ready to give up. It was at that point that I started viewing classrooms as needing to be "nesting grounds" for students. Unfortunately, however, classrooms often do not feel like nesting grounds to black male students. Instead, these students react to the classroom as though they were captives in a hostile environment.

Recently, I observed a reading lesson in an urban middle school in Baltimore, Maryland, that involved five boys and one girl. All of the students were African American. As a pre-reading activity, new vocabulary was being introduced. The teacher held a bell he would use to control the pace of the lesson, and told the students to get ready. He called out the word *Agatha*. The students repeated the word. This process was repeated with the words *Demarco, Adeline, Emilia,* and *pumpernickel.* Then the students took turns reading aloud. The teacher corrected their every miscue: "No, that's not *coastal*, that's *castle*." He then had the students respond aloud to the assessment questions at the end of the text. They provided wrong answers for a majority of the questions. For each incorrect response, the teacher provided the correct answer, but he did not explain why that response was better than the student's. As the lesson wore on, I noticed that the male students appeared uninterested. The whole process was deadening. The students were reading from decontextualized text and were not provided any explicit strategy instruction or word study instruction. They were simply asked to repeat words, read aloud, and answer questions. With activities so unrelated to the students' lives, and their resulting lack of interest, I did not see how being in this particular classroom was going to help these students become better readers.

The classroom I just described is one kind of bad environment that makes students feel trapped. Here is another.

Several years ago I conducted a detailed inquiry in my eighth-grade classroom to determine why four of my black male students were not becoming engaged in our daily reading period (Tatum 2000). Over the course of several interviews the young men admitted that they were afraid to read in class. They blamed derogatory remarks from previous teachers as deterrents to reading. One of the young men stated, "People think that most black people are going to fail, so we don't do the work." Another student stated, "We are not used to reading and writing, it's like we are starting over in eighth grade." To avoid negative comments from a classroom teacher or peers, one of the young men said, many of them would rather say nothing than risk embarrassment. These students' teachers had inadvertently pushed them away from reading and had constructed barriers to their own students' progress.

These two examples reaffirm my point that classrooms must function as nesting grounds for our students. To create such classrooms, teachers must consider the various strands I mentioned earlier: theoretical strands, used in planning instruction; instructional strands, for classroom practice; and professional-development strands, to continually strengthen their own performance.

THEORETICAL STRANDS

Theoretical strands are to the framework for creating nesting grounds what a brain is to a living being: they provide direction for the entire organism. Here's another analogy. If you are planning to provide a meal for a group of foreign tourists, you would first have to decide what kind of meal would be most appropriate for that group. Are there certain dishes that should be avoided? Might they prefer wine with their meal? In essence, you are trying to come up with a menu that has a good chance of satisfying your dinner guests' appetites. In order to do this, you have to know something about your guests' culture; depending on what that culture is, you may have to rethink how you prepare some of your dishes. You may have to make adjustments before rushing out to purchase the ingredients for the meal.

When planning how best to provide literacy instruction to black males, teachers should consider theoretical strands in much the same way as a host would consider how best to entertain foreign guests. There are three theoretical strands for planning instruction that are described in the following pages: reconceptualizing the role of literacy (the focus of this chapter); creating curriculum orientations that empower students (Chapter 5); and using a culturally responsive approach to literacy teaching (Chapter 6).

INSTRUCTIONAL STRANDS

The instructional strands of the framework can be viewed as the midsection—the part of the being that contains many of the vital organs.

These are the strands that have to do with strategy and skill development, the types of texts to use, and the ways to evaluate students' literacy behaviors. Three instructional strands are described in the following pages: using a comprehensive framework for literacy teaching (the focus of Chapter 7); mediating text (Chapter 8); and strengthening assessments (Chapter 9). To use our earlier analogy of preparing a meal for foreign visitors, the instructional strands are akin to the ingredients that one uses to prepare the meal after determining what dishes are most appropriate.

PROFESSIONAL-DEVELOPMENT STRANDS

The professional-development strands are the legs of the framework—they enable us to provide quality literacy instruction that is informed by the theoretical and instructional strands. A teacher can be knowledgeable about both theoretical strands (for example, using a culturally responsive approach to literacy teaching) and instructional strands (for example, using a comprehensive framework to teach reading) and still not be able to use them in a way that leads their black adolescent male students to high academic achievement. In such a case, the professional-development strands must be added. Chapters 10 and 11 focus on professional development: establishing a professional community (Chapter 10) and conducting teacher inquiries (Chapter 11).

To return to our example of a meal for new guests, the professional-development strands would be similar to trying the meal out on your own after you have identified an appropriate menu (theoretical strands) and gotten all of the necessary ingredients (instructional strands), or consulting with someone who has experience with the kind of cuisine your visitors require.

All these strands that make up the framework through which black adolescent males can acquire literacy are shown in Figure 4.1. An initial step in making one's classroom a nesting ground for black male students is to reconceptualize the role of literacy instruction for these students. The focus should be on:

1. Academic excellence.
2. Cultural, social, and emotional development.
3. Authentic discussions related to identity and masculinity.
4. Ways to overcome obstacles.

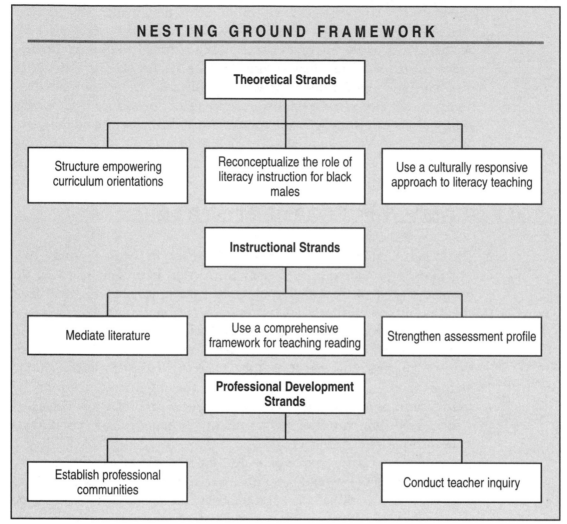

FIGURE 4.1 Nesting Ground Framework

ACADEMIC EXCELLENCE

Black male students—like all students—should be given quality instruction that nurtures their ability to read, write, and think. They should learn how to ask thought-provoking questions and how to analyze written (and non-written) materials in the context of their everyday lives. It is essential that these young men be prepared for higher education and that they not disassociate being smart from being black and male. They must be given opportunities to demonstrate their knowledge. Many of the young men I taught responded to academic challenges when I set excellence as the standard. I would challenge them to answer *every* comprehension-related question correctly, not just some. They responded. I challenged them to read text at their assigned grade level with no miscues. They responded. I challenged them to use the skills and strategies they were taught across the content areas, because it was important for these students to discover that they could attain success in literacy through skill and effort and that they had no innate shortcoming. They responded. The academic challenges I set for my students, backed up with well-planned instruction, allowed these young men to consistently perform well on the end-of-the-year assessments administered to eighth-grade students.

CULTURAL, SOCIAL, AND EMOTIONAL DEVELOPMENT

Black males must learn to resist negative forces in their community that have the potential to destroy their lives. It is often difficult for many of them make it through what I refer to as the "four critical years"—those after middle school and before college. These years are the black male's Bermuda Triangle. Many young men who manage to steer clear of the dangers of these four years wind up with a stronger sense of who they are. They do not feel the need to prove themselves in order to be accepted by other young men if they sense their futures will be placed in jeopardy. Many of the young men who successfully navigate the years from middle school to college attribute their success to self-determination, strength, and an ability to maintain focus on their future. Literacy instruction must nurture such qualities. To accomplish this, teachers need to select texts and plan activities that will foster the development of these students' cultural, social, and emotional literacies. The black male's chances for success are diminished without this development.

AUTHENTIC DISCUSSIONS RELATED TO IDENTITY AND MASCULINITY

As young black males enter adolescence, their sense of identity and ideas of masculinity are connected to their sexuality and the appearance of being tough. This may not be unique to black males, but the stakes for these young men are apt to be higher. Poor black males are disproportionately raised in single-mother households. The absence of a male figure means that many of these young men are on their own in defining what it means to be a man. Oftentimes, they get it wrong. Social service organizations, recognizing the problem of black males growing up without fathers, have urged black men to serve as mentors or big brothers for fatherless boys. Sexual irresponsibility is often overlooked in discussions with students in school, particularly with males in schools where there are few male teachers. This only allows the cycle of fatherless households with young black males to persist.

A misguided notion that being tough is the defining characteristic of masculinity is dangerous for black males. This prevents them from making rational decisions when confronted with life-threatening situations. Many of these young men would rather risk death than be a viewed as a punk. This kind of thinking leads to many premature deaths from black-male-on-black-male crime. The notion of being tough to be a man is corrosive. Unfortunately, conversations about this subject are too often avoided in the classroom.

WAYS TO OVERCOME OBSTACLES

Despite their long history of being disempowered, many black males in America have managed to overcome the obstacles they have faced. Many lessons may be learned from those who have "beat the odds." These lessons can be found in texts, films, and discussions with adult men who are invited to schools to share their success stories. Young black males can learn to take proactive measures to overcome obstacles. Currently, two of my former students are attending a university they visited while they were students in my class. During our class trip, I arranged for the two to talk with black male college students who had come from their community. They were so inspired by the college students, who were only a few years older, that the young men in my class became determined to attend the same university.

Reconceptualizing literacy instruction to address more than academic performance and planning instruction that is responsive to more than academics can seem overwhelming. These things, however, must be done because young black men who must live and learn amid turmoil often find it hard to believe that success is possible. Conversely, it is equally true that wealthy teenage boys have a hard time believing that failure is possible. Tobias Wolff provides an example of this in his novel *Old School*. He describes a young man who is willing to be expelled from school during his senior year. Purcell, who comes from a wealthy family, did not believe graduation really mattered because a high-school diploma would open no doors that weren't already open to him because he was his father's son. He wouldn't even lose his place at Yale.

Many black males living amid turmoil believe that their education does not matter, particularly when they have experienced years in school that seem to them to lack importance. Like Purcell, they believe that there is a place reserved for them, and that a high-school diploma would open no doors to them that are not already open. Unlike Purcell, however, their reserved place is not Yale, nor is it a place offering anything like the same advantages. The doors these black males perceive as being open lead to a dismal landscape—a bleak future.

Going back to Wolff's novel, there is another incident that occurs that bears resemblance to what needs to take place in the literacy education of black males. This is illustrated in the text below:

> *Say you have just read Faulkner's "Barn Burning." Like the son in the story, you've sensed the faults in your father's character. Thinking about them makes you uncomfortable; left alone, you'd probably close the book and move on to other thoughts. But instead you are taken in hand by a tall, brooding man with a distinguished limp who involves you and a roomful of other boys in the consideration of what it means to be a son. The loyalty that is your duty and your worth and your problem. The goodness of loyalty and its difficulties and snares, how loyalty might also become betrayal—of the self and the world outside the circle of blood.*
>
> *. . . You've never had this conversation before, not with anyone. And even as it's happening you understand that just as your father's troubles with the world—emotional frailty, self-doubt, incomplete honesty—will not lead him to set it on fire, your own loyalty will never be the stuff of tragedy. You will not turn bravely and painfully from your father as the boy in the story does, but forsake him without regret. (pp. 5–6)*

In the above example, a teacher selected a text deliberately because he wanted his students to extend the meaning of the text into their own lives. He knew that his students could relate to being a son. By involving his students in a conversation about Faulkner's (1995) text, this teacher helps them understand the nature of the relationship between father and son. He then steers his students to discuss that relationship with other boys in similar situations.

Black males also have relationships that are described in texts. Teachers can use these texts to help their black male students add meaning to their lives even as they enhance their literacy development. Just as it would have been difficult for the teacher in Wolff's novel to help the boys in his class examine their relationships with their fathers if he had used a decontextualized, skills-focused orientation, teachers of black males would have a hard time helping their students examine relationships in their lives with a decontextualized, skills-focused orientation to literacy instruction. Literacy has to be defined more broadly, and more meaningfully, than that. For example, black males should be encouraged to think about the following questions:

■ What does it mean to be a man?
■ What does it mean to be a black male?
■ What does it mean to be a black male in America?
■ What does it mean to be a black male in the global community?
■ What does it mean to be described in animal terms (for example, as an endangered species)?
■ What does it mean to be despised because of the color of your skin?
■ What does it mean to be racially profiled?
■ What does it mean to be placed in the lowest-performing schools?
■ What does it mean to be misunderstood?
■ What does it mean to be feared?
■ What does it mean to be the descendant of an enslaved group?
■ What does it mean to be a citizen in a nation that has not allowed you to be president?
■ What does it mean to be stereotyped as a criminal?
■ What does it mean to be praised just because you speak standard English?
■ What does it mean to have more of your group in prison than in college?
■ What does it mean to have more formal education but make less money than your white male counterparts?
■ What does it mean to be a victim of police brutality more often than any other group?
■ What does it mean to have to fight upstream?
■ What does it mean to overcome?
■ What does it mean to have to justify your presence?
■ What does it mean to have to defend your rights as a human being?
■ What does it mean to be pacified with low expectations?

- What does it mean to be viewed as sexually promiscuous and out of control?
- What does it mean when others are uncomfortable around you?
- What does it mean to be the focus of local, state, and national commissions because of negative social conditions?
- What does it mean to be the representative of all things black and male?
- What does it mean to be invisible?
- When does it mean to have people distrust you because you are black and male?
- What does it mean to have an unbalanced representation in the news and the media?
- What does it mean to have one of the shortest life spans?
- What does it mean to be figuratively feminized and castrated?
- What does it mean to spend years of no importance in schools?
- What does it mean to be endlessly judged and evaluated by European standards?

These questions suggest why a high percentage of black males are undereducated or miseducated in many of America's schools. Many of these subjects appear in daily newspapers and state or national reports that can be accessed on Web sites by the U.S. Department of Labor (www.dol.gov), the U.S. Department of Education (www.ed.gov), the U.S. Department of Justice (www.usdoj.gov), the newly formed State of African American Males (www.saamchicago.org), and the National Urban League (www.nul.org), which provides an annual report on the status of African Americans in the United States. These issues are also discussed in books, such as *Countering the Conspiracy to Destroy Black Boys* (Kunjufu 1987), *The Beast* (Myers 2003), and *The Glory Field* (Myers 1995). Students need not read the entire texts from the sources just mentioned; teachers can identify excerpts that are provocative and relevant.

In addition to print, motion pictures that feature black males can be used to advance the literacies of black males and address the questions listed above. For example, in two relatively recent movies featuring black teenage males living amid turmoil, *Hurricane* (Jewison 2000) and *Finding Forrester* (Van Sant 2000), reading or writing was central to the lives of the black male characters. In *Hurricane*, Lesra, a sixteen-year-old, picked up a copy of *The Sixteenth Round* (Carter 2003), an autobiographical narrative of Rubin "Hurricane" Carter, a black male boxing champion who was imprisoned for murder. After reading the book, Lesra concluded that the boxer was wrongly convicted by America's system of justice, and he became inspired to free Hurricane Carter. He approached the adults who were supporting him and said, "So what are we going to do?" They asked, "Do about what?" He responded, "About Rubin." For this young man, who admittedly had never read a novel, the book he happened to pick up gave him a purpose larger than himself. He discovered the transformative power of reading.

In *Finding Forrester* Jamal, another sixteen-year-old, developed a better understanding of himself through journal writing. He carved out a sacred space for writing that was meaningful to him. His writing became more polished when he met a white male mentor who challenged him to improve. At one point in the movie, the mentor, after reading a particularly well-written piece of Jamal's writing, says to Jamal, "You're sixteen and you're black." Jamal is offended; thinking the comment is a race-based insult, he angrily responds, "What does that mean?" The white male, unafraid to confront racist stereotypes, does not shy away from the question and retorts, "Don't run me down with that racist bullsh—." This character sincerely wanted Jamal to understand more about writing and to become a better writer. The mentor encouraged Jamal to write from a space that mattered. He gave him rich feedback about his writing and acknowledged Jamal's black maleness. Jamal ended up at an elite prep school on a scholarship, partly because his former school, in an impoverished urban area, could not help Jamal adequately identify what he wanted to do with the rest of his life.

In both movies, literacy held power for the young black male characters when it was authentic; when it related to their lives; when it focused on their cultural, social, and emotional development; when it helped them overcome obstacles; when it acknowledged their black maleness; and when it helped them identify what they wanted to do with the rest of their lives.

Literacy development can also be powerful for black males when it acknowledges their current existence while not allowing them to become limited by that existence. Both of the young black males in the films just described harbored feelings of anger, but their anger was acknowledged and confronted. When teachers ignore or invalidate the anger of their black male students, the result can be ongoing tension and resistance.

Lesra and Jamal received support by caring persons who moved them to become active as a result of their literacy, stand up for something larger than themselves, and become more critical readers and writers in the process. The examples of these young film characters can be used to help black male students think about their own literacy development. The films can also cause teachers to examine their role as providers of literacy instruction to black males. In some ways, teachers need to understand their students the way they understand their subject matter. No one can teach mathematics without first understanding mathematics. Similarly, no one can teach black males who must read amid turmoil without understanding both black males and their turmoil.

Teachers' failure to provide instruction that leads black males to read about, write about, and think about important issues related to their existence contributes to their invisibility and demasculinization in school and society. It certainly does little to help them. Currently, many instructional practices are not aimed at removing the "iron cages" that trap black males into the role of the beast in America's belly (Takaki 1990). Educators must reconceptualize literacy and give it new orientations, particularly as it relates to curricula, instruction, and assessment practices. This will not occur if the focus is on standardized test scores and other detours that move us away from quality literacy instruction that is responsive to the needs of black males.

Many young black men will continue to suffer reduced chances for success until their teachers begin to understand that these students want real knowledge from people who care about issues that really affect them. These young people need teachers to walk into classrooms with the aim of teaching their students something new, knowledge that matters. They would respond to teachers who approach them with the conviction "I am going to teach you how to accumulate wealth; how to become empowered politically; how to be healthy; and how to become a man." These are aims that relate to America's unfulfilled promise of equality and inclusion. Young black men feel the sting of the disparities in education, housing, and employment opportunities. They want to know that teachers care about their lives as well as their literacy. One way teachers can communicate this care and commitment is through curriculum orientation.

STRUCTURING CURRICULUM ORIENTATIONS THAT EMPOWER STUDENTS

There is every indication that, in spite of the laws, significant numbers of enslaved black people were trying to learn how to read and write. . . . "Dere was some dat wanted larnin' so bad dey would slip out at night and meet in a deep gulley whar dey study by de light of . . . torches." . . . Collectively, this secret learning represented a people's thrust toward new self-definitions, toward creative transformation of a culture.

Vincent Harding, *There Is a River*

Some large urban school districts, Chicago being one, are experiencing a groundswell of interest in establishing schools operated by private foundations as a means of improving the education of low-income minority students. One local newspaper article stated that 22 Chicago schools must dramatically improve test scores this year or face a state takeover, a reopening as a charter school, or a wholesale firing of staff. Another 242 schools, most of them in Chicago, it was said, would face the same fate in two years if they do not boost test scores (Grossman 2004). The article went on to state that the 22 schools would work on school improvement plans while district officials considered the worst-case scenarios of state takeover, reopening as charter schools, or firing staff.

There is also a move to remove entire teaching and administrative staffs in low-performing schools and replace them with supposedly more qualified teachers and administrators. Under the No Child Left Behind act, all states are required to develop plans to achieve the goal that all teachers of core academic subjects be highly qualified by the end of the 2005–06 school year.

These are the kinds of remedies being proposed to improve students' academic performance. At the same time, there are those who believe that public schools are working and that teachers in public school settings just need more support to address the needs of their students. Both sides, however, agree on one fundamental idea: the need to address questions regarding curricula. These questions can be summed up as follows:

1. What should be taught?
2. Why should this be taught—that is, how is this meaningful for those being taught?
3. What will be the outcome of teaching this?

These three basic questions lead to the examination of curriculum materials, curriculum orientations, and the role of schooling for a particular group of students—in short, the second theoretical strand in the framework proposed in Chapter 4.

SHOULD CURRICULUM BE FUNCTIONAL OR EMPOWERING?

In the epigraph that opens this chapter, education is connected to self-definition and transformation of culture for black people collectively. Questions about the role and choices of curriculum for blacks in the

United States are not new. In fact, at the dawn of the twentieth century these questions were hotly debated by two preeminent thinkers and black spokesmen of their time, Booker T. Washington and W. E. B. Du Bois. While Washington favored a practical education for African Americans and the development of skills that would help them gain entry into the economic mainstream, Du Bois emphasized the need for upward mobility that would help African Americans achieve equal social, legal, and political status in the United States. This debate has yet to be settled.

The positions of Washington and Du Bois were based on the assumption that the African Americans experience in the United States was qualitatively different from that of the rest of the nation. Because the black experience in the United States has included more than two hundred years of chattel slavery, more than eighty years of legal and de facto segregation, and the subsequent negative effects of these experiences, curriculum orientation for this group is often polarized. On one end is a functional orientation emphasizing skill development; on the other, an orientation based on developing intellectual ability. This has created an either–or dilemma for many institutions responsible for educating African Americans.

The latent effects of these two orientations, functional versus empowering, persist in many schools where black adolescent males are being taught. The push to raise test scores has also affected curriculum orientation. The influence of testing on curriculum choices is not without precedent. Herbert Kliebard (1995) described how standardized testing took root as a result of the movement for scientific curriculum making and the rise of social efficiency in the first quarter of the twentieth century. He noted that "the field of curriculum as a distinct area of specialization within the educational world was born in what may be described as a veritable orgy of efficiency, and the after effects have been felt throughout the twentieth century" (p. 81). There is a prevailing tendency in many schools serving economically disadvantaged black male students to focus on rote, basic skills as a way to satisfy the demand for testing (Darling-Hammond 1998). Literacy practices are in turn attuned to testing practices. This can lead to a society where the differentiation of labor into low-skill and high-skill becomes necessary (Galbraith 1996). This has the potential to put students who are not exposed to other orientations of literacy, such as literacy for empowerment, at a disadvantage.

Teachers must eradicate disempowering curriculum orientations and move beyond standardized test instruments and their hold on literacy instruction. Black adolescent males must be taught in a way that extends beyond a skill and strategy instruction aimed at minimum requirements on standardized tests. Linda Darling-Hammond (1998) has highlighted several problems teachers of black students must face:

1. Schools that serve large numbers of African American students are least likely to offer the kind of curriculum and teaching needed to meet high academic standards.
2. Many urban systems have focused their curricula more on rote learning of basic skills than on thoughtful examination of serious literature or assignments requiring frequent and extended writing.
3. African American students' lack of equal access to challenging curriculum and high-quality materials are serious impediments to progress.
4. The National Assessment of Educational Progress (Campbell, Donahue, Reese, and Phillips 1996) pointed out that the kinds of classroom practices associated with higher reading scores—using trade books and literature rather than basal readers and workbooks, encouraging frequent discussions and writing group projects, and having students make presentations—are less likely to be made available to urban and minority students.

In order to avoid disempowering curriculum orientations, teachers should focus on developing an orientation that includes the following:

1. Engaging students with text and discussions about the real issues they, their families, and their communities face, where the students can analyze their lives in the context of the curriculum and discuss strategies for overcoming academic and societal barriers.
2. Using meaningful literacy activities that address students' cognitive and affective domains and that take into account the students' culture.
3. Connecting the social, the economic, and the political to the educational.
4. Acknowledging that developing skills, increasing test scores, and nurturing students' identity are fundamentally compatible.
5. Resolving the either-or dilemma of focusing on skill development or developing intelligence.

In order to structure an effective curriculum orientation for black males, teachers must evaluate present curricula and select quality materials that will engage their black male students and maximize the potential for improved academic, social, and economic outcomes. The emphasis

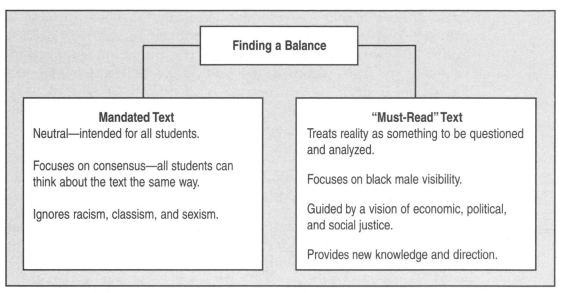

FIGURE 5.1 Finding a Balance

here is on *engagement* and *outcomes*. Often, teachers find that black males will participate in rich discussions of interesting text, but that their performance in these discussions does not necessarily lead to improved academic performance—that is, improved test scores. One practical solution for this problem is to balance mandated texts with "must-read" texts. Figure 5.1 shows some of the differences between the two types of text.

EVALUATING CURRICULUM ORIENTATION

Evaluating curriculum orientation should begin with certain questions.

What Is Happening During Literacy Instruction on a Day-to-Day Basis?

Teachers need to engage in ongoing reflection to determine whether their instruction is meeting the needs of their black male students. Imagine keeping a journal of reflection. In it, you would note the types of texts you used with the students and how they responded to the text; the word study and vocabulary instruction provided; the comprehension strategies taught and how well the students applied them; the highlights of whole-class and group discussion; and your assessment practices and what they revealed. Then imagine taking a step back to reflect on your instructional planning. This will lead you to think about why certain texts were selected in the first place. Examine the goal and focus of the lesson. Examine why you chose to teach a particular strategy. Examine the words you selected for vocabulary development. Then ask yourself what you were trying to accomplish with your instruction. These questions should reveal a lot about the curriculum orientations.

How Is the Curriculum Committed to Advancing Multiple Literacies in the Lives of Black Males?

In addition to thinking about the instruction, you should reflect on your role in providing that instruction. Individual teachers or school staffs can use this question to examine their instructional focus with black males. What are the anticipated outcomes of your instructional focus at year's end? Is the goal to improve students' academic literacies as reflected by test scores? Is the goal to help shape the identities of black males who are living amid turmoil and help them move from the discourse into which they were born? Are students' cultures acknowledged when making curricular decisions in order that your teaching can be culturally responsive? Are the curriculum and the way it is taught generating the conditions for failure or success? Reflecting on these questions will lead you to think about how the lives of black males must inform the instruction that is planned for them.

We need to pay attention to the "stuff" of the curriculum—where knowledge comes from, whose knowledge it is, what societal groups it supports, and so on (Apple 1990). In the end, we should ask two critical questions when examining curricula: Does the curriculum preserve existing inequalities? Is knowledge being unevenly distributed?

If black males are going to be made to face the scrutiny of high-stakes testing and greater accountability and penalized later in life for inadequate literacy development, then the curricula they are exposed to must also face scrutiny. Along with high-stakes testing, black males should receive high-status knowledge—that is, knowledge that is economically beneficial in terms of long run benefits to the most powerful classes in society (Apple 1990). In addition, black males should receive cultural and social benefits from the education they receive. As teachers and administrators select curriculum content and negotiate the meaning of the content, they should also assess how the planned curriculum will address the needs of their students.

"MUST-READ" TEXTS

A recent experience leads me to believe that curriculum orientation is not being held up to keen scrutiny. In a suburban school district in Maryland, during a professional development session that focused on closing the reading achievement gap of black males in the district's schools, I asked the group, "What are the 'must-read' texts for black males?" My question, addressed to a racially diverse audience of more than fifty educators, including district supervisors, building administrators, and teachers, was met with silence.

This question was not one I had planned to ask as I prepared for the workshop. It was stimulated by a conversation with a high school English teacher who approached me while I was in the room setting up. The conversation went something like this:

Teacher: How do I get my students to read the texts?

Tatum: What texts are you asking them to read?

Teacher: We have an adopted literature series.

Tatum: Is there anything about the adopted literature that's a barrier?

Teacher: I'm not sure; they're just not interested.

Tatum: Are there ways you can engage their interest? Is it possible for you to help them understand why reading the selected text is important?

Teacher: What do you mean?

Tatum: Why do you want the students to read the materials? Why *must* they read the materials?

Teacher: If they don't read, they won't become better readers.

Tatum: I agree. But is there something unique or magical about the materials they are required to read that will help them become better readers? Or are there other materials that they can read that will help them become better readers?

Our conversation was forced to end as the other workshop participants entered the room. My reason for asking the question about must-read texts was to find out whether this group's black male students and their specific needs were being considered when curricular decisions were made.

To stimulate a response to the must-read texts question during the workshop, I began to name some must-read texts for black males from a historical perspective. I mentioned the following:

- The alphabet
- Their names
- The Bible
- Manumission documents
- The Emancipation Proclamation
- *Appeal: To the Coloured Citizens of the World* by David Walker
- *The Narrative of the Life of Frederick Douglass, An American Slave* by Frederick Douglass
- *Up from Slavery* by Booker T. Washington
- *The Miseduccation of the Negro* by Carter G. Woodson
- *The Autobiography of Malcolm X* by Alex Haley and Malcolm X
- *Invisible Man* by Ralph Ellison
- *Go Tell It on the Mountain* and *The Fire Next Time* by James Baldwin
- *Native Son* and *Black Boy* by Richard Wright
- *A Raisin in the Sun* by Lorraine Hansberry

This prompted two responses from the participants. One teacher mentioned two books by Walter Dean Myers, *Slam!* and *Monster*. These two fictional works are appropriate for middle school students, but can also be used in a high school English course. An administrator said that the texts I mentioned as being historically important were still must-read texts for black males. He added that his son, who was in his mid-twenties, was reading one of the books and was finding the book relevant today, although it was written more than twenty years ago.

Below is a list of other must-read texts I would recommend for black males reading amid turmoil. Most of them can be used as "cultural hooks" to engage black male students. My list is in no way exhaustive; I do not mean to suggest that these are the only must-read texts for black males. Beyond these recommended texts, black males need exposure to a vast array of fiction and nonfiction texts across genres, as suggested by Carol Collins (1993).

- *The Pact: Three Young Men Make a Promise and Fulfill a Dream* by Sampson Davis, George Jenkins, and Rameck Hunt
- *There are No Children Here* by Alex Kotlowitz
- *A Hope in the Unseen: An American Odyssey from the Inner City to the Ivy League* by Ron Suskind
- *The Beast* by Walter Dean Myers
- *Our America: Life and Death on the South Side of Chicago* by LeAlan Jones, Llyod Newman, and David Isay
- *The Greatest* by Walter Dean Myers

- *Letter to My Nephew* by James Baldwin
- *Stories of Scottsboro* by James Goodman
- *Workin' on the Chain Gang: Shaking off the Dead Hand of History* by Walter Mosley
- *Think Big* by Ben Carson
- *And Still We Rise: The Trials and Triumphs of Twelve Gifted Inner-City Students* by Miles Corwin

One teacher mentioned that long books, similar to the ones offered as must-read texts, are automatic turn-offs for her students. She made the point that it is difficult to guide students through a lot of pages in meaningful ways when the students find little or no value in the material. She added that students are intimidated by texts with high page counts. This frequently causes a dilemma: the students' resistance is dealt with by allowing them to read fewer pages. This "accommodationist approach" results in black males reading less, rather than more. Thus, teachers are partly responsible for black males' literacy remaining underdeveloped.

A better solution to this problem is to have black males read more texts that address their concerns and texts that can help shape their ideas and their identity. The volume of text black males read can be increased if they are given text that matters to them.

In retrospect, I wish I had asked the teachers in the professional development session to identify key issues they should focus on in attempting to close the achievement gap in their county. I would have asked them a few questions to stimulate their thinking, such as the following ones taken from Bakari Kitwana's (2002) *The Hip Hop Generation*:

- How is the worldview of young male and female blacks different from those of previous generations?
- How have high incarceration rates affected the lives of young blacks?
- Why do the unemployment rates of young blacks remain twice as high as those of their white counterparts?
- What does it mean to come of age in postsegregation America?
- How has coming of age in an emerging global economy influenced the worldview of blacks?

Kitwana asserts that "these questions—the answers to which begin to explain this generation's career choices, relationships, education, music, politics, activism, and lifestyle—probes the roots of the crises that now threaten to envelop us" (p. xxii). If teachers do not examine these and other important issues, and if they fail to analyze the problems in a broader context so as to inform their attempts to close the achievement gap, their attempts are likely to be ineffective.

SHORTER TEXTS AS A BRIDGE

To address the teacher's concern about the length of the texts I originally offered as must-read texts, I suggested shorter alternative texts as one way to get students into eventually reading lengthier texts. The idea is to use the alternative text as a bridge to the longer text, not as a replacement for it. For example, a few years ago for a ninth-grade classroom, I used an article from a local newspaper as a springboard to *Kaffir Boy* (Mathabane 1986), a longer text that was required reading. I also used the shorter text as a way to build the students' knowledge about science. The article was entitled "'Dr. Death' to Testify in Apartheid-Era Trial" (Figure 5.2).

The following is the lesson plan I developed:

Objectives
- Students will be able to define apartheid and tell of its geographic location.
- Students will learn about some of the horrors of apartheid.
- Students will increase their knowledge about forms of warfare.
- Students will discuss the positive and negative uses of science.
- Students will suggest reasons for African Americans to be knowledgeable about science.

Important Vocabulary
1. apartheid
2. fatal
3. human rights
4. chemical warfare
5. biological warfare

Before the Reading
Discuss science.

Create a pros and cons chart of science (see Figure 5.3).

Create a semantic map of forms of warfare (see Figure 5.4).

Introduce key vocabulary.

Model self-questioning strategy using first two paragraphs of the newspaper article.

"DR. DEATH" TO TESTIFY IN APARTHEID-ERA TRIAL

By Susanna Loof
THE ASSOCIATED PRESS
AP

JOHANNESBURG, South Africa—Witnesses have talked of creating poisoned chocolates and clothes, lacing a letter with anthrax and releasing cholera in the water supply at a refugee camp.

Wouter Basson, the so-called "Dr. Death," took the stand on Monday to face questions about the chemical- and biological-warfare program he headed under South Africa's apartheid regime.

It was to be the first testimony by Basson, whose 21-month-old trial on charges of murder, fraud and drug trafficking has reminded South Africans of the horrors of apartheid.

Testimony has included accounts of salmonella sugar and an experiment where naked blacks were smeared with a gel to test whether it could kill, and allegedly injected with fatal doses of muscle relaxants and dumped in the ocean when it didn't.

As the head of the secret program that allegedly searched for ways to kill black enemies of the state during apartheid, Basson, a cardiologist, traveled the world under false identities to gather information, funds and materials. Prosecutors say he supported a luxurious lifestyle by siphoning state money from companies set up to hide the operations.

Basson angered many South Africans when he refused to apply for amnesty from the country's Truth and Reconciliation Commission, which would have required him to tell all in public hearings. His trial now is seen as a symbol of what happens to those who ignored the commission's effort to find out the truth about apartheid-era crimes.

"The Basson case demonstrates very clearly what the nature of the apartheid state was . . . a criminal state that was involved in really major schemes of mass and serious violations of human rights," said Shadrack Gutto, a lawyer at the Center for Applied Legal Studies at the University of the Witwatersrand in Johannesburg.

Basson, who has pleaded innocent to all charges, will not talk to the media, his attorney Jaap Cillier said.

The presiding judge dropped 15 of 61 charges last month without explanation, including allegations Basson tried to kill Reverend Frank Chikane by poisoning his clothes. Chikane is now President Thabo Mbeki's chief of staff.

Basson was also cleared of the gel-smearing killings, but he still faces 13 murder charges.

The Pretoria High Court was evacuated several times during the trial after anonymous callers threatened to blow up the court if the case was not adjourned.

Journalists beset the trial as it opened in October 1999, but public interest quickly faded as lawyers began arguing about the complex web of front companies and international links that hid Basson's alleged fraud.

The trial attracts only occasional attention, such as when bacteriologist Mike Odendaal testified last year he had freeze-dried HIV-infected blood for use against enemies as part of Basson's program.

Basson has remained calm throughout the trial, said Marlene Burger, who is observing the trial for the Center for Conflict Resolution.

"He shows no emotion of any kind. He and his legal team are very arrogantly confident that he will be acquitted," she said.

That Basson, who rose quickly in military ranks, became such a key figure demonstrates how the apartheid system was run by normal people persuaded by a perverted idea, Gutto said.

"The apartheid state really used very normal ordinary professionals with otherwise good standing from an academic-intellectual level," Gutto said. "It was not a system that was really run by sick people. These were normal people."

Seeing democracy approaching, F.W. de Klerk—the last apartheid president—forced Basson to retire in 1992, but Basson was rehired during Nelson Mandela's presidency. The new government said it had to rehire Basson to prevent his knowledge from ending up in the wrong hands.

But his comfortable life began to crumble when he was arrested in 1997 for allegedly selling Ecstasy to a police informant. Basson's program allegedly manufactured large quantities of street drugs, supposedly for crowd-control purposes.

Investigators found documents in Basson's home detailing the chemical- and biological-warfare project known as Project Coast.

The find led to Truth and Reconciliation Commission hearings on the project and many of the charges against Basson.

Basson, who is free on bail, continued to practice medicine at a government hospital until May, when he was forced to retire.

Prosecuting and defending Basson is likely to cost South Africa more than the $5.6 million he is accused of pilfering, Burger said, adding that the trial is worth any price.

"[The state] has done the right thing because of what he's been accused of doing," Burger said.

FIGURE 5.2 "Dr. Death" Article. Copyright © 2005 Associated Press. All rights reserved. Distributed by Valeo IP.

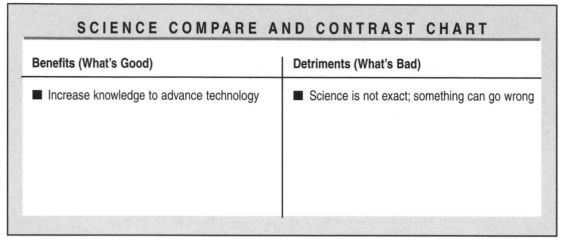

FIGURE 5.3 Chart: Pros and Cons of Science

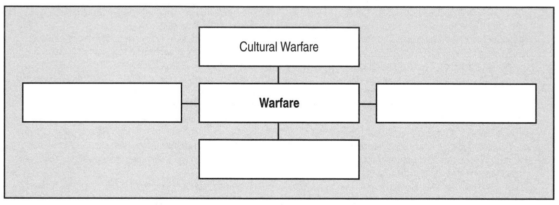

FIGURE 5.4 Semantic Map: Forms of Warfare

During the Reading
Self-questioning and annotation

- Students will identify the key characteristics of each paragraph and create a question that is answered by each paragraph (self-questioning strategy).
- Students will construct a question when something is unclear (comprehension monitoring).

After the Reading
Discuss implications of science contextualized within apartheid.

Revisit pros and cons.

Discuss other forms of warfare.

Complete examples of chemical warfare and biological warfare.

Draft one paragraph about the reasons for African Americans to be knowledgeable about science.

I copied the first sentence in the article onto a transparency to stimulate a pre-reading discussion:

> *Witnesses have talked of creating poisoned chocolates and clothes, lacing a letter with anthrax and releasing cholera into the water supply at a refugee camp.*

To model self-questioning, I added two questions to the transparency:

1. How can someone create poisoned chocolates and poisoned clothes?
2. Why is this happening?

As reflected in the lesson plan above, this shorter text can accomplish several things. It introduces students to a concept central to the subsequent, longer reading: the treatment of blacks in South Africa, a major theme of *Kaffir Boy*. Also, the students are given explicit instruction on self-questioning strategies and comprehension monitoring. Word study is contextualized into the article. And the students are asked to think about reasons African Americans specifically should be knowledgeable about science. During one point in the post-reading discussion, I asked the students whether they thought African Americans should have to rely on the goodwill of others if they are subjected to some of things mentioned in the newspaper article, or whether they should be able to protect their own interests.

This lesson focused on more than skills and strategies. The students were constructing knowledge and were becoming motivated to read *Kaffir Boy* with a keen, and newly developed, interest in apartheid. Several of the students asked if the information in the article was true. They did not believe it was possible. Two months after the class read the article, the attack on New York's World Trade Center occurred. The word *anthrax* soon became more than just a word in a pre-reading exercise: there was a real anthrax scare in the United States. I would have loved to have another conversation at that point with the students who read the article about Dr. Death. I suspect they recalled our lesson in the days and weeks after 9-11.

For lessons like this to occur requires that teachers develop a better understanding of the wide variety of texts that exists and how these texts can be used to help black males examine their lives both inside and outside of school. When selecting texts for your students, consider the many kinds of literacy in their lives. Select texts that are cognitively demanding. Select text that allows your students to apply the skills and strategies you have taught. Select texts that may help students structure their lives in a way that will keep them from contributing to their own failure. Don't make your students identify main ideas in texts if you have determined, based on meaningful interactions with the students, that the main ideas in those texts do not matter to them.

Nontraditional texts may be selected to complement existing curricula and to create a bridge for your students. Newspaper or magazine articles, news clippings, electronic documents, song lyrics, movie dialogue, essays, books, plays, and literature anthologies are all viable options. Access to the Internet makes the task easier. For example, if you want your students to examine the relationship between economics and increased prison rates—how it has become profitable to incarcerate black males—you could select an article from the Internet about the privatization of prisons. Some years ago I used the following excerpt from an article as a way of getting a group of students interested in a chapter on economics in their social studies textbook. (The entire article can be found at http://www.corporatewatch. org/magazine/issue11/cw11f6.html.)

Prison Privatisation

The current prison system in the UK is <u>imported</u> from America, one of the few countries with a higher proportion of its population behind bars than the UK. Many of the same companies are involved. These companies are paid per inmate per day so the more people locked up, the more money they make. Private prisons hold people for longer than state prisons and lobby the Government for harsher sentences.

In the UK more people are being sent to prison and sentences are getting longer. The prison population has been rising since 1993, when it was 45,000, to its current figure of around 65,000. At the same time, a massive prison building program has been underway involving three prisons currently under construction, three more planned, and extensions to existing prisons.

Five more prisons for young people are planned to cater for the 2,500 extra 10 to 19 year olds expected to be locked up at any one time as a result of the Crime and Disorder Act. From April 2000 the Youth Justice Board will deal with all places for 10 to 19 year olds.

Wackenhut is almost entirely owned by its founder, George Wakenhut, ex-FBI agent and multimillionaire. George Wackenhut made his fortune building files on civil rights activists and <u>anti-war</u> <u>protestors</u> and selling the information to anyone with the money to pay. By 1965 he had files on 2.5 million Americans.

In November 1999 Wackenhut was profiting from more than 38,600 people behind bars and had plans to expand to take 9,000 more.

Corrections _Corporation_ of America (CCA)

Corrections Corporation of America (CCA) specialises in prisons. It was founded in 1983 by an advisor on corrections for the Governor of Tennessee, the national president of the America Correctional Association, and the _investors_ behind Kentucky Fried Chicken. CCA finances, designs, constructs, renovates and manages prisons in the US, Puerto Rico, Australia and the UK. CCA has been accused of abusive treatment of prisoners and inadequate healthcare. Three inmates at CCA's prison in Youngstown, Ohio have sued the company for abuse and failure to protect them from staff and other inmates.

Last year the Colorado Department of Corrections investigated CCA's Kit Carson prison over allegations that guards were involved in drug smuggling and brutality. The warden was put on administrative leave and guards were charged with bringing contraband into the prison. So many of the staff quit or were fired that CCA was offering guards bonuses of $100 to recruit friends and family with a further $100 if the new recruit stayed for 3 months.

CCA's _share_ _value_ has risen from $8 in 1992 to $30 in 1997. It is so proud of itself that it posts its _daily_ _share_ _index_ on the gates of its prisons.

The underlined words were discussed during vocabulary development because they were part of the social studies chapter. I selected this article because it was useful for mediating a discussion on the interconnectedness of economics, politics, and crime and also related to a plague of incarceration being faced by the community where the lesson was taking place. Afterward, I showed the students how to read the stock pages in the newspaper to extend their knowledge about share values. I wanted to demonstrate to them the need to study economics because their community was part of an economic equation whether the students realized it or not.

Often I chose text that emphasized the collective responsibility of black males to uplift their communities. I would connect these materials to the existing English language arts and social studies curricula. Three short poems—"Lineage" by Margaret Walker, "I Too" by Langston Hughes, and "America" by Claude McKay—can be used this way (African American Literature 1998). The poems by Langston Hughes and Claude McKay follow.

I Too

I, too, sing America.
I am the darker brother.
They send me to eat in the kitchen
When company comes,
But I laugh,
And eat well,
And grow strong.
Tomorrow,
I'll be at the table
When company comes.
Nobody'll dare
Say to me
"Eat in the kitchen,"
Then.
Besides,
They'll see how beautiful I am
And be ashamed—
I, too, am America.

America

Although she feeds me bread of bitterness,
And sinks into my throat her tiger's tooth,
Stealing my breath of life, I will confess
I love this cultured hell that tests my youth!
Her vigor flows like the tides into my blood,
Give me strength erect against her hate.
Her bigness sweeps my being like a flood.
Yet as a rebel fronts a king in state,
I stand within her walls with not a shred
Of terror, malice, not a word or jeer.
Darkly I gaze into the days ahead,
And see her might and granite wonders there,
Beneath the touch of Time's unerring hand,
Like priceless treasures sinking in the sand.

The discussion of these texts centered on the love-hate relationship many black males have with America. The poems hold the message that black men have the ultimate responsibility of determining their own fate—"eat well," "grow strong" in the Hughes poem and "I stand within her wall with not a shred of terror" in McKay's poem. The students and I revisited these themes throughout the course of the school year. I selected these texts for my black male students in an attempt to prompt them to make connections between who they were (the past), who they are (the present), and who they would become (the future).

Focusing on black male empowerment and, perhaps, the part they play in their own disempowerment during literacy instruction is an effective way to engage black males with text. Providing them with an outlet for expressing their views about issues critical in their lives can also be effective. Although its authenticity is debatable, I often used the text of a speech supposedly written by Willie Lynch to stimulate my middle school students' writing and thinking. Lynch, a British slave owner in the West Indies, was said to have delivered this speech in 1712, having been approached by American slave owners for a solution to keep their slaves under control. Lynch asserted that his plan, if implemented, would last for many hundreds of years. (The underlined words are vocabulary words I placed on the word wall in my classroom.)

Gentlemen, I greet you here on the bank of the James River in the year of our Lord one thousand seven hundred and twelve. First, I shall thank you, the gentlemen of the Colony of Virginia, for bringing me here. I am here to help you solve some of your problems with slaves. Your invitation reached me on my modest plantation in the West Indies where I have experimented with some of the newest and still the oldest methods of control of slaves. Ancient Rome would envy us if my program were <u>implemented</u>. *As our boat sailed south on the James River, named for our illustrious King, whose version of the Bible we cherish, I saw enough to know that your problem is not* <u>unique</u>. *While Rome used cords of woods as crosses for standing human bodies along its highways in great numbers you are here using the tree and the rope on occasion.*

I caught the whiff of a dead slave hanging from a tree a couple of miles back. You are not only losing valuable stock by hangings, you are having uprisings, slaves are running away, your crops are sometimes left in the fields too long for maximum profit, you suffer occasional fires, your animals are killed. Gentlemen, you know what your problems are: I do not need to <u>elaborate</u>. *I am not here to* <u>enumerate</u> *your problems, I am here to introduce you to a method of solving them. In my bag here, I have a foolproof method for controlling your Black slaves. I guarantee every one of you that if installed correctly it will control the slaves for at least three hundred years. My method is simple. Any member of your family or your overseer can use it.*

I have outlined a number of differences among the slaves: and I take these differences and make them bigger. I use fear, distrust, and <u>envy</u> for control purposes. These methods have worked on my modest plantation in the West Indies and it will work throughout the South. Take this simple little list of differences, and think about them. On top of my list is "Age", but it is there only because it starts with an "A": the second is "Color," or shade; there is intelligence, size, sex, size of plantations, status on plantation, attitude of owners, whether the slave live in the valley, on hill, East, West, North, South, have fine hair, coarse hair, or is tall or short. Now that you have a list of differences, I shall give you an outline of action—but before that I shall assure you that distrust is stronger than trust and envy is stronger than <u>adulation</u>, respect, or admiration.

The Black slave after receiving this <u>indoctrination</u> shall carry on and will become <u>self-refueling</u> and <u>self-generating</u> for hundreds of years, maybe thousands. Don't forget you must pitch the old Black male vs. the young Black male, and the young Black male against the old Black male. You must use the dark skin slaves, vs. the light skin slaves and the light skin slaves vs. the dark skin slaves. You must use the female vs. the male, and the male vs. the female. You must also have your white servants and overseers distrust all Blacks, but it is necessary that your slaves trust and depend on us. They must love, respect and trust only us. Gentlemen, these kits are your keys to control. Use them. Have your wives and children use them, never miss an opportunity. If used <u>intensely</u> for one year, the slaves themselves will remain <u>perpetually</u> distrustful. Thank you, gentlemen. (Lynch 1712)

I asked my students to examine Lynch's timeline and explore the concepts of *self-refueling* and *self-generating*. I asked whether any among us were guilty of participating in his plan. I also asked whether there were any members of our family (meaning my classroom) who were guilty. These struggling middle school students, who were reading two to three years below grade level, were being exposed to rich vocabulary, critical thinking, and text that caused them to think about their situation in the world and their relationships with each other. Following the discussions, I asked my students to write a response to Lynch's letter. One black male student's response (Tatum 2000) reads as follows (the underlined words were pulled from the word wall):

The Man

I am the black man who ashames his race.
I am the darker brother whom they laugh in my face.
I have many disadvantages that bring me down.
I fight the power when I know it's not allowed.
Feeling the walls close on to my position in the center of the earth.
Hoping to make peace inside of the man's world feeling the
    dehumanization coming from the man who awaits my death.
Making me weak on the inside, taking over my soul,
taking my true love from me, left with nothing to hold.
Lost within myself this can't be real,
can not stand this antithesis of life I feel.
Growing darkness taking dawn I thought was me, but now I'm gone.
I have awaited my life too long to let the man pull my arm.
Seeking chaotic episodes happening everyday
feeling the critters in my head moaning stay away.
Having my manhood stripped away from me everyday.
Having no respect for society, because I know I must turn away.
Running away from my fears all alone.
There's no way in the world I can be strong, but I must,
because it seems as if my whole race is depending on me.
Walking around with unknown attributes. Scared to face the world's
    prevaricating nations.
Hiding from the intimidation that awaits me at home.
Feeling the products of lethal weapons growing strong.
The source that kills my brothers and sisters I know it's wrong.
I know now I must lend my brothers and sisters a hand, and hope
they learn the true meaning of overcoming The Man.

This student examined the turmoil he was experiencing and placed it in the context of the nation. He doubtless was influenced by the intertextual connections we made in class. Reading and text selection were rarely isolated. I tried to connect the texts to my students' lives and use them as a bridge to help my students read and understand the textbooks, which contained valuable information and were, after all, useful for helping students meet high academic standards.

I believe I learned to use texts in this way by the curriculum orientations I received as a student attending a low-achieving school in an urban public school district. My eighth-grade teacher required that the students in our class read and memorize the poems "Invictus" and "Test of a Man," both of which contained the message that our choice to become or not to become resided within. He had us read the newspaper every day and complete a current-events assignment during our lunch hour, when we had to identify the journalist's five W's (who, what, when, where, and why) for each article. He was teaching us to put our minds in contact with local, state, and national events. He was nurturing us to think about contexts larger than our own. I also recall my sixth-grade teacher, who made us carry index boxes filled with cards with multisyllable words. During her instruction, she used words that she knew would not be found on standardized assessments administered to sixth-grade students. She refused to limit her teaching to the tests. For example, I remember her requiring us to define the word *euthanasia* and debate its merits because it was at the time the subject of national discussion.

Similar to the concept of motivating males to read by selecting texts that help them "fix their Chevys" (Smith and Wilhelm 2002), black males can be motivated by curriculum orientations aimed at "fixing their lives." By saying this I do not mean to suggest that something is broken; what I mean is that their education should focus on helping them improve their chances to become economically, intellectually, and politically visible in the society in which they live. I want students to connect to text the way I connected with Dick Gregory's autobiographical novel, *Nigger*.

Black males living amid turmoil need to develop strategies and hope for overcoming academic and societal barriers. Such strategies will cause them to search for meaning in their lives and will help them construct their visibility. They will find the strength to challenge the status quo; they will be able to break through their turmoil. If these opportunities are not made available to them in the curriculum and the instruction they are exposed to, black males will just be exposed to "school stuff" that is of little use to them. Teachers who succeed with their black male students resist a sole focus on "school stuff"; they use a culturally responsive approach to literacy teaching. They understand that their students should get the knowledge they deserve, that schools must work for all students, and that curriculum orientation matters.

CHAPTER 6

A CULTURALLY RESPONSIVE APPROACH TO LITERACY TEACHING

The crippled veteran of the Pacific war says to my brother, "Resign yourself to your color the way I got used to my stump; we're both victims." . . . Nevertheless with all my strength I refuse to accept that amputation. I feel in myself a soul as immense as the world, truly a soul as deep as the deepest of rivers, my chest has the power to expand without limit. I am a master and I am advised to adopt the humility of the cripple. Yesterday, awakening to the world, I saw the sky turn upon itself utterly and wholly. I wanted to rise, but the disemboweled silence fell back upon me, its wings paralyzed.

Frantz Fanon, *Black Skin, White Masks*

n the chapter of his book *Black Skin, White Masks* entitled "The Fact of Blackness," Frantz Fanon recalls how his brother was advised to accept his color as an injury. His brother was being instructed to accept the status of victim because of his skin color. The amputee equated his condition to that of a black man. However, Fanon refused to view his race and culture as deficits, embracing instead his power to expand without limit. Unfortunately, these things are too readily seen by others as crippling, and these attitudes are what prevents him from rising.

FACETS OF CULTURE

Culture consists of the ever-changing values, traditions, social and political relationships, and worldview created, shared, and transformed by a group of people who are bound together by a combination of factors (Nieto 1999). These factors can include a common history, geographic location, language, social class, and religion. Culture is dynamic; it is not limited to the historical traditions and cultural artifacts that are so often taken as a group's culture, and it goes beyond stereotypes to include variations within a group. Sonia Nieto (1999) explains,

> *Culture is complex and intricate; it includes content and product (the what of culture), process (how it is created and transformed), and the agents of culture (who is responsible for creating it and changing it). Culture cannot be reduced to holidays, foods, or dances, although these are, of course, elements of culture. . . . Everyone has a culture because all people participate in the world through social and political relationships informed by history as well as race, ethnicity, language, social class, gender, sexual orientation, and other circumstances related to identity and experience. (p. 48)*

What this means is that black males living amid turmoil may be different culturally from black males who live free of turmoil. Although there is a common *historical connection* for all black males in America, the *culture* of young black males may depart as a result of social class and other related experiences. A few years ago, I read a book entitled *Our Kind of People: Inside America's Black Upper Class* (Graham 2000), which chronicles the lives of the black elite. The author, who grew up in such a family, recalls that his mother would often take him on summer trips to communities where poor blacks lived and tell him that he was responsible for helping those people out. He notes that he took these trips in the 1970s, and mentions being taken to a specific neighborhood in Chicago. As I continued to read, I realized that my neighborhood was one of this writer's field trips. We were both young black American males of approximately the same age, but our culture was extremely different. This young black man felt that he was responsible for helping "unfortunate" young people—meaning me! Though our race and history were shared, our culture was clearly not the same. This is why the term culture must be examined critically.

CULTURE AND EDUCATIONAL ACHIEVEMENT

There has been endless discussion of the impact culture has on students' educational achievement. Competing educational theories offer differing views. At one end of the spectrum is the notion that societal factors affect educational achievement. With regard to black males, for example, how this group is treated in the wider society is said to be reflected in how they are treated in the educational system. With this perspective, it follows that black males respond to schooling based on both their perception of the treatment they receive in school and their perception of what schooling will do for them in the future—their return for investment in schooling, as it were.

An eighth-grade student once asked me why I talked so much about the need to go to college. He said, "I know a lot of men with college degrees who are unemployed or still living at home with their mothers because they don't make enough money." I replied that the mere fact of having a college degree does not lead to success, but being smart does. I told the young man that when I speak of college, I am not speaking of the credential; I am speaking of college in a broader sense, as an institution where a wide body of knowledge is accessible. I acknowledged that it is true that college degrees have not granted equal access for black males to all that America has to offer (for example, the presidency of the United States or CEO positions of *Fortune* 500 companies); but I told him that for every man he could name with a college degree who was not working, I could name ten who had college degrees who *were* working. I concluded by saying that I, for one, am very glad that I did not have to figure out what to make of my life without a college degree and the knowledge I gained at college, but added that it is, of course, up to him to decide about college. Looking at broader societal issues can help educators understand why some students behave—and believe—the way they do: they often tend to follow group-patterned behavior (Ogbu 1998).

Another school of thought relating culture to education has less to do with broad economic, political, and social considerations; it focuses on smaller, more specific day-to-day realities. This perspective focuses on the relationships between home culture and school culture, student-teacher interaction patterns, and teacher instructional practices and assessment strategies. Considering culture in this way may reveal differences in cultural values, knowledge, and practices between black male students and their teachers, and that these differences are related to the young men's chances for success. In order to prevent or minimize conflict between black males and their teachers, a culturally responsive approach to literacy teaching should be used.

CULTURALLY RESPONSIVE TEACHING

A culturally responsive approach involves teachers' using their students' culture as an important source of the students' education. Gloria Ladson-Billings (1995) argued for the centrality of a culturally responsive approach for helping students who have not been served well by our nation's public schools, and asserted that teachers create conditions for effective learning when they recognize the importance of culture and make use of students' culture in specific activities. However, one should not assume that all students from the same cultural background learn the same way.

Although few studies have examined the relationship between culture and education among adolescents, it is clear from the available research that using an instructional approach disconnected from students' culture creates student resistance. (See, for example, Foster 1997; Hale 1994; Hollins 1996; Hudley 1995; Lipman 1995; and Tatum 2000; 2003.) To understand the impact of culture in an adolescent's life, keep in mind that attaining a sense of identity is a central concern of adolescence. Young people formulate their identity both inside and outside of school. Many adolescents acquire cultural knowledge and a richness of expression outside of school only to find that these facets of their self-identity are neither recognized nor used in school. Teachers and students must learn how to navigate whatever cultural differences exist in a respectful way and in an atmosphere of mutual trust. The existing research also suggests that students' opportunities to learn increase when teachers conduct lessons in a culturally responsive manner consistent with community values and norms for interaction. For black adolescent males, in order to offset resistance that occurs because of cultural differences and to help develop their identities, it is essential to establish culturally responsive instructional practices and infuse the curriculum with culturally relevant materials. In this way these young men will not view their lived experiences outside of school as being marginalized inside it.

The kinds of materials that have been found to be most effective in the classroom are those containing authentic portrayals that students can identify with—including characters, settings, and situations, or themes that students are keenly interested in and that are relevant to students' lives (Henry 1998). Other classroom materials that are effective with adolescent students of minority groups are those that provide them with multiple opportunities to create links between the text and their prior knowledge and ideas. Young adults appreciate interesting reading material that makes sense to them (Au 1993; Harris 1993). Texts should reflect reality, but they should also point the way to a different, and better, reality (Collins 1993).

Literacy instruction that pays attention to the needs of black males and acknowledges their turmoil can be regarded as culturally responsive. Geneva Gay (2000) lays out a good description of culturally responsive teaching. She informs us that it:

1. Acknowledges students' cultural heritage as it affects their dispositions, attitudes, and approaches to learning, and recognizes that it contains content worthy to be included in the curriculum.
2. Builds meaning between students' home and school experiences as well as "school stuff" and the students' lived realities.
3. Uses a wide variety of instructional strategies.
4. Teaches an appreciation of the students' own cultural heritage as well as that of others.
5. Incorporates multicultural information, resources, and materials in all subjects and skills routinely taught in schools.

Two Teachers' Experiences

Consider the experiences of two teachers as they attempted to use a culturally responsive approach to literacy teaching.

Teacher 1

The first teacher, an African American woman, taught in an upper elementary classroom in a low-achieving school in a large urban school district. She was born and raised in the South and had a strong sense of racial pride.

She vividly recalled (and often shared with me) memories from the civil rights era and the experiences she had had with her father, who was a proud black man. This teacher was very caring toward her students. She would come to school early and stay late. She would give her students money if they asked her and she felt they urgently needed it. She had a wonderful rapport with the students' parents. Pictures of African American heroes and heroines lined the walls of her classroom. In addition, she would sometimes wear traditional African garb. She would often tell stories about her upbringing in the South and about the challenges African Americans faced in the past. She used cultural idioms familiar to the students in her speech. You would often hear her verbally reprimanding her students if they stepped out of line. She was no-nonsense and demanded respect from her students at all times. The students seemed to like and respect her.

However, this teacher's instruction yielded substandard achievement results. On some days, there was more storytelling in her classroom than instruction. There was a lot of off-task time. The skill and strategy instruction she provided was poor. It was not uncommon for her to misspell some words that she wrote on the chalkboard, and she had difficulty solving some math problems she was responsible for teaching. She would tell her students, "See? Teachers don't know everything." But teachers need to know the content they are responsible for teaching. This teacher was falling short. Although she was culturally sensitive and created a caring classroom community, her instruction did not lead her students to high academic achievement.

Teacher 2

The second teacher, like the first, taught in the upper elementary grades. He had been raised in the community where he taught. He dressed in a suit most days, for two primary reasons, he said: he wanted students to understand that he took his teaching and everything about it seriously; and he wanted the students to have an image of a black male not commonly seen in their community. In the rear of his classroom was a bulletin board that listed the "Afro-Bets." Each letter of the alphabet was associated with the name of a successful African American. For example, C was assigned to Ben Carson, who was head of neurosurgery at John Hopkins Hospital in Baltimore, Maryland. M was assigned to award-winning writer Toni Morrison. This teacher consciously decided to use the names of living people to demonstrate to the students that African Americans continue to make major contributions, and that important African Americans are not just vestiges of the past. In the front of his classroom was a sign that read "Join the 9.0 Club." This was an exhortation to the students to achieve at least a grade-equivalent score of 9.0 on the required standardized assessment test that was administered near the end of the academic year. This sign was displayed prominently even though a majority of the students had entered his classroom reading several years below grade level, and were required by the school district to achieve a grade-equivalent of 7.0 to earn promotion to high school.

This teacher greeted the students at the door each day. Upon entering the room, the students readied themselves to go to work right away. It was clear that an instructional routine was in place. During the lessons, the teacher gave explicit strategy instruction. Before-reading, during-reading, and after-reading activities were planned. He demanded that students read text fluently. He would say to students who repeated words or phrases while reading aloud, "If you see it once, say it once." The teacher told students beforehand to avoid making miscues (repetitions, substitutions, and omissions), and they were encouraged to self-assess their reading behaviors. The students were made to provide evidence for their responses when answering comprehension questions; this teacher was more concerned that the students demonstrate their understanding, not just answer questions correctly. This also allowed the teacher to assess students' reading performance more fully. He demanded excellence.

The students read from an anthology of African American Literature (1998); they also read novels that reflected their culture (for example, *Roll of Thunder, Hear My Cry* by Mildred Taylor, *Cousins* by Virginia Hamilton) and some that did not (Lois Lowry's *Number the Stars* and *The Giver,* Karen Cushman's *The Midwife's Apprentice*). This teacher encouraged the students to make intertextual connections, as well as connections to the students' own lives and experiences. This teacher referred to the students as "Sir" and "Ma'am." He occasionally sat among his students in a circle in the middle of the classroom during reading instruction. The room had a feeling of community. Outside the classroom, the teacher could be observed playing basketball with his male students and jumping rope with the female ones. At the end of each year, the students participated in a play that they wrote with the teacher. The plays were always designed to reflect on the African American experience in America. Many of the students, who became better readers and thinkers under his tutelage, considered this teacher the best they ever had. Many of these students had "hated" this teacher at the beginning of the school year for being too tough.

Elements of Success

The portraits just presented of these two teachers suggest that a culturally responsive approach entails more than dressing a certain way or interacting with students in a caring manner. The two teachers dressed differently, each for different reasons; both treated their students with respect. A culturally responsive approach to teaching is more than just helping students become more familiar with their culture or making them feel good about themselves, though both teachers did these things, one teacher by shared stories and the other by teaching the Afro-Bets. A culturally responsive approach goes beyond knowing about the students' community and using familiar cultural idioms, and it's not about having students love you because you are kind and fun to be with. Although your students should come to trust that you have their best interests at heart, it is more important that they be receptive to instructional approaches targeted toward excellence.

By design, a culturally responsive approach to literacy teaching gives explicit attention to academic excellence as well as cultural competence. It is not simply an infusion of cultural facts or a display of cultural artifacts that highlight the rich and storied past of African Americans and their contributions to the world. It goes further and deeper than that. Thinking that the goal is simply to make students feel good about themselves without concern for academic achievement and competence in reading and writing is a fundamental misconception. Rather, a culturally responsive approach to literacy teaching expands what students are exposed to, and challenges teachers to do whatever is within their power to help students embrace high expectations for themselves and to help them reach those expectations despite what others outside the classroom—parents, siblings, peers, other teachers and administrators, a racist society—might expect of them.

Teachers who use a culturally responsive approach with their black male students understand their own culture in relationship to that of their students. They recognize that the failure of black boys in school does not truly represent who these boys are; instead, these teachers view failure or low levels of achievement as obstacles to overcome with committed, quality teaching. Culturally responsive teachers are reluctant to acquiesce to the idea that black boys living under stressful conditions have a legitimate excuse not to perform well. They are able to check their assumptions or misconceptions about what it means to black and male in the United States.

In 1994, while I was teaching in a K–8 school, Gloria Ladson-Billings' book *The Dreamkeepers* was published. Her description of culturally relevant pedagogy reminded me of both my own teaching practice and that of my own middle school teachers years earlier. Ladson-Billings' book also convinced me that all culturally responsive teachers are not the same. She provided portraits of both black and white teachers who provided culturally responsive instruction to black students. Her book answers the question "Do you have to be black in order to provide culturally responsive instruction to black male students?" In short, the answer is no. The characteristics of the teaching are more important than the characteristics of the teacher.

In a later work, Ladson-Billings (2002) describes an incident with Shannon, a young African American girl, and her teacher. Shannon is sitting with three white students in a group as they are trying to think of a sentence that describes something special they did over the weekend.

> *"What did you do last weekend, Shannon?" asks Audrey.*
>
> *"Oh nuttin'," replies Shannon. Denny and Keith agree that the table should choose Denny's sentence to write. Shannon remarks to Keith, "You always choose his sentences!" Keith says, "We don't pick your sentences 'cause you're too grumpy!" Shannon snaps back, "I don't want no White people pickin' on me!" There is an eerie silence and then the other children settle down to begin writing. Shannon only writes the word "I" and begins to complain that she cannot write the word "grandma."*
>
> *After a few minutes one of the teachers comes by the table and notices that Shannon is just sitting while the others are working at constructing the sentence. "Would you like to try writing your sentence today, Shannon?" Shannon shakes her head no, arises from the table and begins to wander around the room. The teacher says to her as she begins wandering, "That's okay. Maybe you will feel like writing tomorrow." (p. 110)*

After providing this anecdote, Ladson-Billings wondered whether some teachers were allowing children to fail. She also wondered whether these teachers were allowing children to fail because these youngsters' cultural style, form of language, and attitudes were deemed by their teacher to be unworthy. These attitudes are not characteristic of culturally responsive teachers, as described in her earlier works. According to Ladson-Billings, "culturally relevant teaching is designed to help students move past a blaming the victim mentality . . . and it is well thought out, careful and reflective practice undergirded by a commitment to the students' academic achievement, their cultural competence, and their socio-political consciousness" (pp. 111, 112).

How close are you to being a culturally responsive teacher? Consider the following checklist. Culturally responsive teachers:

- Know their students and the subject matter they teach.
- Place learning in a meaningful context.
- Help students understand more about themselves and more about the world.
- Find ways to help students see the implications texts have for their lives, futures, and communities.
- Provide instruction that gives shape and form to students' lives.
- Use literature that is culturally relevant and that speaks to their students' experiences.
- Help students understand society's perception of who they are while helping students define who they want to become.
- Avoid using a social efficiency model of literacy instruction just to get through the day.
- Pay attention to current events and incorporate them into lessons.
- Apprentice students toward success.
- Establish classroom communities based on the concepts of care and culture.
- Establish trusting relationships and feelings of kinship.
- Address the multiple literacies in students' lives (academic, cultural, developmental, emotional, and social).
- Understand the lived experiences of their students and how their students respond to these experiences.
- Connect, as best they can, students' in-school lives with their out-of-school lives.
- Understand their role as being broader than just helping students do well on tests.
- Emphasize cooperation over competition during instruction.
- Have knowledge of students' cultural history and the residual effects of that history.
- Carry the burden of success with their students, not assigning success or failure to the students only.
- Understand cultural-specific behaviors.
- Plan instruction and assessments with a rich audit of who the students are.

- Confront racist stereotypes in the curriculum and the instructional environment.
- Understand that literacy can be a tool of resistance.
- Help students critique the cultural norms and mores in society.
- Resist curriculum orientations that are disempowering.
- Seek ways to make intertextual connections.
- Focus instruction on helping students develop strategies and hope for overcoming academic and societal barriers.

Culturally responsive pedagogy has been effective for addressing the literacy needs of students of color. However, policy makers, school administrators, and classroom teachers have not called for its widespread implementation as a way to promote the reading achievement of black males. Gay (2000) enumerates five reasons for this:

1. There is a belief that education has nothing to do with culture and heritage.
2. Too few teachers have adequate knowledge about how teaching practices reflect European American cultural values.
3. Many teachers want to do their best for all their students and mistakenly believe that to treat students differently because of their cultural orientation is a form of racial discrimination.
4. There is a belief that good teaching is transcendent—identical for all students and under all circumstances.
5. Education is claimed to be an effective doorway of assimilation into mainstream society for people from many diverse cultures, ethnic groups, social classes, and points of origin.

My own middle school teachers understood the need for something beyond best reading practices; they understood the need to be culturally responsive. They used empowering curriculum orientations and selected texts they believed would lead me to become actively engaged with reading. They did not use a single set of strategies. They saw literacy instruction as a tool of resistance. The approach they used was similar to my own approach to teaching and the approach used by other effective teachers. Within a culturally responsive framework for literacy teaching, the curriculum, the students, the teaching, and the assessments all matter.

Understanding a culturally responsive approach to literacy teaching and the two other theoretical strands offered in the previous chapters enhances teachers' potential for increasing the reading achievement and addressing other literacy needs of their black male students. But awareness of these theoretical strands, though essential, is not sufficient. Needed also is knowing how to effectively teach reading strategies, ways to organize discussion, and assessment approaches that can be used to plan responsive teaching.

CHAPTER 7

USING A COMPREHENSIVE FRAMEWORK

A traveler in ancient Greece had lost his way and, seeking to find it, asked directions of a man by a roadside who turned out to be Socrates. "How can I reach Mt. Olympus?" asked the traveler. To this Socrates is said to have replied, "Just make every step you take go in that direction."

Eric Butterworth, *Discover the Power Within You*

As I run my fingers across the spines of a bookstore's wares and pick up books in a wide range of topics, I often think about black males who never avail themselves of this knowledge, who are dispossessed from the liberating practice of reading. It is unfortunate that many of these young men never come in contact with texts that can elevate them to levels they have yet to imagine for themselves. Using the lyrics of singer Marvin Gaye, they have no idea of "what's goin' on" between the pages of a book. Oftentimes, they lack the requisite skills and strategies. These young men need quality literacy instruction that moves them toward the ability to read and understand a large variety of texts as they move through adolescence into adulthood. In this chapter, I offer a comprehensive framework of literacy teaching aimed at this goal.

A comprehensive framework of literacy teaching includes, at minimum, the following components: word study and vocabulary development; fluency instruction; comprehension instruction; and writing instruction. In good schools—schools that work for all students—there is consistently high-quality classroom instruction that attends to these components (Allington and Cunningham 1996). These components are based on existing research on best literacy practices and are closely related to literacy practices recommended in the report from the National Reading Panel (NICHD 2000). Like that report, this chapter focuses more on reading practices than writing practices, although the connection between reading and writing will be addressed.

A comprehensive framework of literacy instruction for black males, however, extends beyond research-based practices: it should be anchored in the theoretical strands discussed in Chapters 4, 5, and 6. Unfortunately, most efforts to improve the reading achievement of black males use a skill and strategy approach uninformed by other considerations. This may be one of the reasons why many black adolescent males resist instruction and choose not to complete high school. Such instruction is not enough for black adolescents who have lived amid turmoil and suffered from neglect in American classrooms for years. It is for this reason that I believe that a comprehensive framework of literacy teaching should do at a minimum two key things for black males that extend beyond skill and strategy instruction. It should provide transformative ideas that have the potential to change these young men's lives, and it should superimpose ideas of meaningful living over feelings of surrender.

PROVIDING TRANSFORMATIVE IDEAS

Skills and strategies are only working tools; they have little utility for advancing students' literacy. They are similar to providing a student with a hammer and nails: simply giving someone a hammer and nails does not mean that the person will come up with the idea of building a house. In the unlikely event that the person does think of using the equipment to build a house, he or she will also need apprenticeship or additional supports in order to maximize the likelihood that the house will be built with a solid foundation. With a good foundation, the house will provide its builder with warmth and comfort. The hammer and nails alone do not lead to shelter, but the possibilities presented by the hammer and nails, and the accompanying apprenticeship, do.

When teachers give their black male students skills and strategies without also showing them the transformative possibilities associated with those skills and strategies, the students will find them to be useless tools. This is what happens, for example, when teachers use test prep in an attempt to improve students' reading scores. Many students in the class, not just black males, are likely to ask the question "Why are we doing this?" They may also complain, "We did this already." If teachers are unable to make the skills and strategies they teach relate in some way to their students' lives, the students will not see the need to use the skills and strategies. They are more likely to use what the teacher gives them when they discover that it can be used for a wide range of possibilities in their out-of-school lives. When young black males see that the skills and strategies can be used to build knowledge that empowers them, they will come to value these things and believe in their utility. This is important for black males living amid turmoil, who may not believe in the value of school because of their day-to-day reality. It is difficult for them to see, for example, how a self-questioning strategy and comprehension monitoring are useful if the texts they are asked to question or comprehend are without meaning for them.

SUPERIMPOSING IDEAS OF MEANINGFUL LIVING

Many young black males surrender their life chances, before they come to believe there are options other than failure. If this happens, it is difficult to convince them that such things as reading fluently, making inferences, improving vocabulary, and writing well matter. These literacy goals have to be embedded in texts that mean something to these young men. By the time black male students reach middle school and high school, they want to know how improved literacy will benefit them. This is particularly true of the young men who do not envision college in their future. It is not enough to tell them "I am going to teach you how to comprehend text, read fluently, increase your vocabulary, and become better writers" without helping them see how these things can improve their lives.

I have a fifteen-year-old nephew who lives in one of Chicago's notorious west-side neighborhoods. He flunked sixth grade three times and was promoted to the eighth grade because of his age without ever completing the seventh grade. He then failed eighth grade and was required to go to summer school and meet a minimum requirement on a standardized test if he wanted to move on to high school. His summer instruction was grounded in test preparation activities aimed at the minimum requirements needed for promotion.

My nephew's skill and strategy instruction was disconnected from anything that addresses his real-life turmoil. He is wrestling with the idea of dealing drugs and dropping out of school. He recently told my sister-in-law that he would not return to school as an eighth grader. He feels embarrassed because his younger sister is about to enter eighth grade. The form of instruction he has received has not helped him. His teachers simply believed that if the same skill and strategy instruction were repeated he would be able to meet the minimum requirements for graduation. The text they used did not matter to him, and his experiences did not matter to them. Now this young man is ready to surrender.

Michael Eric Dyson (2004), a young black male from an inner-city Detroit ghetto, describes this experience of black male surrender in a letter to his brother:

Letter to My Brother, Everett, in Prison

The passion to protect ourselves from criminals, and the social policies which that passion gives rise to, often obscure a crucial point: thousands of black men are wrongly imprisoned. Too many black men are jailed for no other reason than they fit the profile of a thug, a vision developed in fear and paranoia. Or sometimes, black men get caught in the wrong place at the wrong time. Worse yet, some males are literally arrested in their development where, if they had more time, more resources, more critical sympathy, they could learn to resist the temptations that beckon them to a life of self-destruction. Crime is only the most conspicuous sign of their surrender.

I guess some, or all, of this happened to you. I still remember the phone call that came to me announcing that you had been arrested for murder. The disbelief settled on me heavily. The thought that you might have shot another man to death emotionally choked me. I instantly knew what E. B. White meant when he said the death of his pig caused him to cry internally. The tears didn't flow down his cheeks. Instead, he cried "deep hemorrhagic tears." So did I. (pp. 20–21)

Dyson provides a cultural and social critique of the imprisonment of black males and their surrender to penal institutions. Their surrender is in large part connected to an arrested development resulting from their inability to resist their social conditioning. Dyson's critique ends with the emotional pain that causes one to cry internally. Dyson's text reminds me of James Baldwin's (1963) "Letter to My Nephew" in both title and form. In both letters, the authors use figurative language to drive their point home to the reader. Dyson's choice of language—"arrested in their development, "death emotionally choked me," "deep hemorrhagic tears"—is well crafted.

Dyson credits his ability to write so meaningfully to others who taught him the importance of words and ideas found in books. He recalls that his schooling functioned as a nesting ground. He was exposed to literature. His teachers held high expectations for his success. They taught skills and strategies in meaningful contexts. Instruction must prepare black males to express themselves in articulate ways, ways that will allow them to call up ideas that will help them formulate critiques like Dyson does in this excerpt. Students in middle school and high school are capable of this kind of writing, as reflected in the students' responses to the Willie Lynch letter, described in Chapter 5.

These two key concepts, providing transformative ideas and superimposing ideas of meaningful living over surrender, suggest that word study instruction and vocabulary development should give students access to words that will allow them to comprehend text they can use as a lever for change. Decontextualized word study should be avoided, because it makes students simply memorize words without giving them a sense of the words' significance. Strategy instruction and skill development must be contextualized. The words and ideas students are asked to engage with must have additional benefits beyond an ability to decode words accurately, read with expression, and read at a pace appropriate for the text type. Students will not achieve those skills if their teachers simply focus on skill and strategy knowledge.

STRENGTHENING CONCEPTS OF READING

As a starting point for using a comprehensive framework of literacy teaching, teachers need to strengthen students' concepts of reading. I learned this during my second year of teaching, when I asked a group of eighth-grade students to explain what I expected of them when I asked them to read. Out of a group of 33, not one student could provide a sufficient response about the reading process. They defined reading as:

- Being able to say the words.
- Reading and answering questions.
- Being able to read without messing up.
- Reading with expression.
- Reading is fundamental.
- Being able to read fast.

After hearing these "definitions," I was determined that this would never happen again with my students—that they would know what it means to read. They should not interpret it as:

- Read the first word and go on until you reach the last word.
- Read in order to answer questions at the end of the chapter.
- Read and then wait for the teacher to ask questions to assess your comprehension.
- Decode all the words correctly.

All of these interpretations imply that reading is a passive process that does not require any action by the reader.

Soccer and Reading

I recall a comment made to me by a student who was enrolled in a developmental reading class at a community college where I taught. She said, "I never viewed reading as an active process; I think about soccer as being active. I don't think of reading the same way I think of soccer. I'm active at soccer practice." I asked her to explain how she gets ready for soccer practice. She replied, "I put on my gear, get the ball, and go out to the field." I probed further.

Tatum: What gear?

Student: My shorts and shin guards.

Tatum: Why the shorts?

Student: They make movement easy.

Tatum: Okay. Why the shin guards?

Student: They're for protection.

Tatum: I see. You can move easy and you have some protection. What do you expect when you go out on the field?

Student: To practice.

Tatum: To practice what?

Student: The routines we use to prepare for other teams.

Tatum: What if your routines are interrupted by your opponents?

Student: I'll do something different.

Tatum: Why do something different? You have routines. You know what to expect in a soccer game, right?

Student: Things don't always work out as planned, so you have to do something else if you want to score goals.

Tatum: Soccer does seem pretty active. You gear up to make yourself comfortable. You protect yourself. You have expectations when you go out to the practice field. You practice routines that have a purpose. You make decisions to do something different if there are things standing in the way of your goals.

I then addressed the entire class, telling them that soccer practice can be used as a way to think about becoming actively engaged with text. With both activities, you must do the following:

1. Make yourself comfortable beforehand by setting expectations, or a purpose. In reading, you might scan the text for difficult vocabulary, or words that you could say might cause pain.
2. Practice or use the skills and knowledge you already possess to help you succeed—in the case of reading, your aim would be to understand text.
3. Be willing to do something different when you encounter obstacles.

In other words, students need to be engaged before the reading (that is, they must decide on a purpose and make themselves comfortable), during the reading (they must monitor comprehension the way they monitor the moves of an opponent), and after the reading (they must determine whether they reached the goal they set out to reach). Students should come to interpret engaged reading as:

- Setting a purpose for reading.
- Constructing meaning of the text using multiple cueing systems.
- Becoming actively engaged with text by monitoring comprehension as they read.
- Assessing their understanding after the reading.

Fluky Flan

To strengthen students' understanding of the reading process, I present them with what I call the Fluky Flan text:

Fluky Flan flubbed and flanned without fubbing. He slipped on a blute and broke his sark. He was rushed to a hod in a sneed that ran every red light. Fluky Flan no longer flubs or flans due to his binny.

Then I proceed with the lesson:

Tatum: Can I get a volunteer to read this?
Student 1: (*Decodes the text accurately.*)
Tatum: Okay, class, how would you say the student read this text?
Student 2: He read it good.
Tatum: Anyone else?
Student 3: I agree, he got all the words right.
Tatum: Anyone else?
Student 4: He read it right.
Tatum: How do we determine if someone's reading is right?
Student 5: They know all of the words and don't mess up.
Tatum: Anyone else?
Student 6: They stop at the end of a sentence when they see a period. You know, they pay attention to the punctuation marks.
Tatum: Okay, let's answer the following questions:
　1. Who is the text about?
　2. What was Fluky doing?
　3. What did he slip on?
　4. Why does he no longer flub or flan?

The students come up with the following responses:

1. Fluky Flan.
2. Flubbing and flanning.

3. A blute.
4. Due to his binny.

Tatum: How do you know the text is about Fluky Flan?

Student: It's right there at the beginning of the sentence. Plus, his name is capitalized.

Tatum: What is flubbing and flanning?

Student 7: I don't know. Those aren't real words.

Student 8: I know! He was running and jumping.

Tatum: Running and jumping? Where does it say that?

Student 8: He had to be doing something to slip. So I say he was running and jumping.

Tatum: What is a blute?

Student 9: Banana peel?

Tatum: Where do you see that? How do you know it's a thing and not an action like flubbing and flanning?

Student 10: Because an action word wouldn't fit right there. It wouldn't sound right if I said he slipped on a jumping. That wouldn't make sense.

Tatum: So reading has to make sense? How do we know if our volunteer who read the text made sense of the text?

Student 11: You did not ask us if he made sense. You just asked how he read it.

Tatum: And one of you said, "He read it good." And someone else said, "He read the text right because he knew all of the words and didn't mess up." But let's move on to question 4. What is a binny?

Student 12: Is this another trick question? If we say "binny" you are going to ask us what's a binny. If we say something else, you are going to ask us more questions.

Tatum: You answered the four questions correctly. I am just asking you to explain your responses. Before we move forward, I want each of you to rewrite the text in your own words, substituting the nonsense words with real words.

I give the students a few minutes to write. Then I resume the discussion.

Tatum: Can I get volunteers to share their responses?

Student 13 (*reads*): Fluky Flan *was running* and *jumping* without *falling*. He slipped on a *rock* and broke his *nose*. He was rushed to a *hospital* in an *ambulance* that ran every red light. Fluky Flan no longer *skates* or *plays* due to his *accident*.

Student 14 (*reads*): Fluky Flan *was running* and *jumping* without *thinking*. He slipped on a *crack* and broke his *ankle*. He was rushed to a *hospital* in a *car* that ran every red light. Fluky Flan no longer *runs* or *jumps* due to his *injury*.

Tatum: Thanks for sharing your rewrites. Do you mind if I discuss them?

Students 13 and 14: Go ahead.

Tatum: Okay, are both of the rewrites correct?

Student 14 (*defending the solution*): I would say the second one is and not the first one.

Tatum: Why? They're both in your own words. Does it matter what words are substituted?

Student 14: The second one makes sense from beginning to end. He slipped and broke his ankle so he no longer runs or jumps due to his injury. In the first one, he broke his nose. That wouldn't stop him from skating or playing. And plus, the words changed from the first sentence. If it's "running and jumping" in the first sentence then it should be "runs and jumps" in the last sentence.

Tatum: Well, let me ask another question. How were you able to put that into your own words?

Student 15: Well, we know that an ambulance or a car runs red lights. And if people get hurt they go to a hospital. Also, we know what words should be action words or not.

I developed the Fluky Flan text to help students understand that good readers rely on graphophonics, or visual cues (the ability to decode the text); syntax, or structural cues (the way the words are positioned in the text); semantics, or meaning cues (the meaning of the text); and schema (the background knowledge they bring to the text). When I asked for a volunteer to read the text with nonsense words I was bringing the students' attention to graphophonics, or visual cues. The first two questions—Who is the text about, and what was Fluky doing?—were designed to help students use syntax and structural cues. Having the students rewrite the text moved their attention to semantics (meaning cues) and schema (background knowledge).

Following this activity, I have students create a small "desk map" that I have laminated and taped to the corner of their desks. They remind the students of the characteristics of good readers:

Good readers:

1. Understand reading as a meaning-making process.
2. Use multiple cueing systems (visual, structural, meaning, and background knowledge).
3. Put text in their own words to check comprehension.
4. Understand that reading is more than answering questions correctly.
5. Read fast enough to make sure they connect the beginning of the text with the end of the text.

TEACHING STUDENT RESPONSIBILITY: THE PLEDGE OF ALLEGIANCE

Once students' understanding of the reading process is strengthened, they must realize that they are responsible for examining text and teasing out its significance. Students—particularly black males living amid turmoil, who must learn to use literacy as a tool of uplift and empowerment—must understand that if they wait for others to help them extract meaning, it may never occur. They should not allow themselves to become victimized by someone else's neglect or unwillingness to help them look deeply into text. To illustrate this point, I use a lesson involving the Pledge of Allegiance.

Tatum: How many of you know the Pledge of Allegiance?

Student 1: We all know it. We've been saying it every day since kindergarten.

Tatum: Okay, take out a sheet of paper and write the Pledge of Allegiance. As you write it, I want you to underline the words *pledge, allegiance, republic, indivisible, liberty,* and *justice.*

I allow a few minutes for the class to write; then I continue.

Tatum: May I have a volunteer to write the Pledge of Allegiance on the board? (*A pause; no one volunteers.*)

Brave student: Forget it, I'll do it. What y'all scared of? (*He writes.*)
I plead allegiance to the flag of the United States of America and to the republic for with it stands one nation under god indevisable with liberty and justice for all.

Tatum: Thanks for volunteering. I needed you today. This class does not work if we do not all participate. Let's give our family member a hand to show how much we appreciate his efforts. (*A bit of applause.*) Now I want each of you to look at the Pledge I have just placed on the overhead projector and make any necessary corrections to the words I asked you to underline and the punctuation. Tomorrow, I will ask you to write the Pledge again, but tomorrow there will be no mistakes. Right, class? (*Some students respond and some do not.*) *Right, class?* (*This time, more respond than not.*) After you copy the Pledge of Allegiance, I want you to answer the following questions so that we can discuss them.

I write the questions on the board:

1. What is *allegiance*?
2. Have you heard the term *republic* before? What does it mean?
3. What is *indivisible*?
4. Why was God placed in the pledge? What does this suggest about this nation?
5. Why have you and many other students been required to say the Pledge of Allegiance each day in school?

The first part of this lesson ends with a discussion of students' responses to the questions. I then tell the students not to say anything in our classroom without investigating the meaning behind it. I also tell them that when they say words in the classroom, they are required not only to know how to pronounce the words, but also to be able to spell them, define them, and use them in multiple contexts.

I then ask the students, who are in the eighth grade, why they never investigated the meaning of the Pledge of Allegiance, which they have been reciting daily since kindergarten. They blame their teachers: "Our teachers never asked us to." I then repeat the question: Why haven't *you* investigated the meaning of the text? I want to make the point that they have a responsibility for their own learning. I then ask for a volunteer to write the words *pledge, allegiance, republic, indivisible, liberty,* and *justice* on the word wall.

EXPECTATIONS FOR HANDLING TEXT

These two lessons—the one involving the Fluky Flan text and the one on the Pledge of Allegiance—I use to set expectations for my students' handling of all texts. I want them to understand what will go on in our class:

- They will be required to actively participate in their literacy development.
- Their vocabularies will be nurtured.
- They are responsible for their own learning.
- They will have the opportunity to fail and recover.
- They will write.
- They will be challenged and supported in a caring environment.
- They will be required to investigate the meaning of text as it relates to their lives.

In the remainder of this chapter I share instructional activities I have used that help students pay attention to each component of the comprehensive framework of literacy teaching, with the exception of writing. There is nothing magical about the strategies. What is important is that teachers use and integrate a core group of strategies consistently so as to increase students' ability to comprehend text. I selected these particular strategies in response to the students' strengths and needs, which I identified using a variety of ongoing assessments. These strategies have helped the black males I have taught over the past ten years.

Figure 7.1 presents the framework for lesson preparation and assessment I have used to anchor my instructional plans (Tatum 2004). It ensured that I paid attention to before-reading activities, during-reading activities, and after-reading activities. It also helped ensure that my instruction was knowledge driven (as opposed to test driven), that it would help increase students' awareness of their performance, and that it would address multiple skills and strategies. Once a usable framework is in place, you can move on to develop activities for improving students' decoding abilities, building their vocabulary, nurturing their reading fluency, and improving their comprehension skills and strategies. In the remainder of this chapter I describe activities I have found to be effective.

IMPROVING DECODING AND BUILDING VOCABULARY

Although there are, of course, a variety of approaches for helping older students decode text and enhance their vocabulary, I describe four that I found especially helpful for the young men I taught. All four are developmentally appropriate for adolescent students. All use text at the students' assigned grade level, *not* their reading level. I found that students were challenged by the high expectations inherent in these instructional

FRAMEWORK FOR LESSON PREPARATION AND ASSESSMENT

1. Is your curriculum choice
   - Developmentally appropriate?
   - Socially and culturally appropriate?
   - Academically appropriate?
   - Emotionally appropriate?
2. How does the text you selected
   - Engage students?
   - Lead to meaningful application of knowledge or skills taught?
   - Tap into students' lives?
   - Engage students' background knowledge?
3. What do you expect your student(s) to learn?
   - Content knowledge
   - Reading strategy/skill
   - About decoding
   - About writing
   - Vocabulary knowledge
   - Other
4. What pre-reading strategies will be used?
   - Building schema (How?)
   - Making predictions (Based on what? E.g., title, first paragraph, other source, etc.)
   - Previewing questions to establish purpose
   - Using anticipation guides
   - Other
5. What form of guided practice will be used?
   - Thinking aloud
   - Modeling
   - Providing written examples
   - Constructing graphic organizers (e.g., K-W-L chart, list, character perspective chart, etc.)
   - Constructing questions
   - Monitoring comprehension
   - Other

6. What will the student(s) be expected to do independently?
   - Demonstrate reading strategy/skill (individually or as a group?)
   - Answer comprehension questions (individually or as a group?)
   - Construct a graphic organizer (individually or as a group?)
   - Construct a written response (individually or as a group?)
   - Other
7. How will you reinforce content knowledge and/or reading strategies/skills after the guided practice and independent practice?
   - Oral explanations will be given.
   - Written examples or graphic organizers will be discussed or reviewed.
   - Correct answers will be provided.
   - Other
8. What type of feedback will each child receive about
   - Use of reading strategy?
   - Decoding ability?
   - Writing?
   - Content knowledge?

   For each, decide which type of feedback to use:
   - Whole-group feedback.
   - A score.
   - Individual information about strengths and weaknesses provided in writing.
   - Individual information about strengths and weaknesses given orally.

FIGURE 7.1 Framework for Lesson Preparation and Assessment

activities: syllabication, oral dictation, word wall work, and semantic mapping (Tatum 2000).

Syllabication

Before incorporating the syllabication activity in our daily routine, I had noticed that my students were struggling with the multisyllable words in the texts they were required to read. They had difficulty identifying the syllables. I decided to give them four simple rules that would allow them to see the word parts and thus help them decode the words. The guiding analogy was "If they attack the small puppies, they will get to the big dog." I told the students that if they could identify the letters *a, e, i, o,* and *u,* and count to 2, they could decode a large number of multisyllable words. I gave them four rules for syllabication:

1. Split two consonants between vowels (e.g., *bal-lad*).
2. When one consonant appears between vowels, it belongs with the next syllable (e.g., *te-na-cious*).
3. Separate neighboring vowels (e.g., *jo-vi-al*).
4. Do not separate blends or word groupings that need each other (e.g., *ous, qu*).

I designed the syllabication activity to help students decode multisyllable words from texts they were expected to read independently. I also selected words for daily syllabication in response to patterns of miscues I detected from students' oral reading. For example, if I noticed that several of the students were having difficulty with words beginning with double consonants (e.g., *pneumonia, gnostic*), I would select words with double consonants to call attention to them and to help students learn how to handle them. The daily syllabication was also a way to help students who knew phonics and had had repeated exposure to phonics instruction to learn how to use this knowledge in an instructional environment that was fast-paced.

Oral Dictation

Oral dictation was another part of my daily instructional routine; it occurred immediately after the syllabication or word wall work. I would dictate two to four sentences, selected to provoke students' interest, inspire thought, or give them information relating to the text we would discuss during the lesson. Often, I used sentences from the first paragraph the students were going to read as part of that day's lesson. Daily oral dictation thus served four purposes: it functioned as a pre-reading activity; it nurtured reading fluency; it improved students' spelling; and it helped me plan subsequent word study instruction.

I told my students to write the sentences verbatim and underline eight preselected words that I would use to assess their spelling. After each dictation, I would score the students on the number of correct words they spelled out of ten—the eight preselected words and the first two words used in the exercise. I began each dictation with the words *revolution* and *responsibility*. Every day I would begin the dictation with the following sentences:

- "The *revolution* begins in the year 2010, so arm yourself with intellect and the passion to create change." (The year 2010 was the projected year the members of the class would finish graduate school and become leaders in their respective professions.)
- "It is your *responsibility* to take care of yourself, your family, and your country."

The other eight words I selected to emphasize common spelling patterns or to call attention to essential vocabulary in the text used during instruction. Following each dictation, we would highlight mistakes and discuss spelling patterns. The same dictation would be used for two consecutive days, and only the second day's score was recorded. Students thus knew that they could fail and recover. They also knew that I expected them to have no errors on the second day.

When I began this exercise, I noticed that some students would not even attempt to spell the words. This was a problem, because if they wrote nothing I could not assess their needs. Therefore, I crafted a developmentally appropriate spelling scaffold to move my students toward participation. I gave them copies of a blank dictation sheet containing lines and boxes. I told them that consonants go on the lines and vowels go in the boxes. I explained that they were all required to take a stab at the words, and I went on to tell them that the scaffold would be removed the next day, when they would be given the same dictation. For example, Figure 7.2 is a spelling scaffold for the following dictation:

People usually associate the word prejudice *with intolerance of a particular race or creed. Prejudice can also exist, however, within a minority group that is the victim of discrimination.*

People ☐ _ ☐☐ _ _ ☐   ☐ _ _ ☐ _ ☐☐ _ ☐ the word

_ _ ☐ _ ☐ _ ☐ _ ☐ with ☐ _ _ ☐ _ ☐ _ ☐ _ _ ☐ of a

_ ☐ _ _ ☐ _ ☐ _ ☐ _ race or creed. _ _ ☐ _ ☐ _ ☐ _ ☐ can also

exist, however, within a _ ☐ _ ☐ _ ☐ _ ☐ group that is the victim of

_ ☐ _ _ _ ☐ _ ☐ _ ☐ _ ☐☐ _ .

FIGURE 7.2 Spelling Scaffold for Dictation

In this way, my expectations for these struggling adolescent readers were not lowered. Instead, I gave them a scaffold to support them as they read and wrote challenging text. The spelling scaffolds were removed when the students no longer needed them.

I always asked several questions afterward that related to the dictated exercise and that the class discussed as a pre-reading activity. For the sentence above, for example, I might ask the following questions:

1. Can you explain why some members of a racial or ethnic group might be given special treatment?
2. What circumstances lead to discrimination?

I would ask volunteers to reread the dictated sentences—or to *reiterate* them (a word I would use to help the students build their vocabulary)—and respond to the questions before we went on to read the selection. Having students read the dictated exercise nurtured reading fluency. I knew the students would see the dictated sentences in their assigned reading for the day.

Word Wall

To strengthen students' vocabulary, both sight and meaning, I set up a "word wall" across several walls in the classroom. The words selected for study I took from assigned texts. I would tell the students that they would find the words on the word wall in their reading; I wanted to be sure they would make the connection. Using text selections to teach word meanings is more effective than assigning vocabulary words at random.

My purpose in designing the word wall was to help my students strengthen the relationship between knowing words and reading well. I used the words on the wall to address decoding and vocabulary simultaneously. Students need to hear and see new words repeatedly if they are to remember them and use them in writing. I also used the word wall as a decoding and spelling scaffold. For example, I would underline parts of words to help students decode words by analogy. I might write the word *spacious* on the word wall with *–cious* underlined. Then, if the students encountered the words *efficacious* or *tenacious* during their reading, they would know that the end of these words is read the same way as the end of *spacious*.

I would ask students to decode a selected portion of the word wall every other day to build their sight vocabulary. I might quote lyrics from songs as associations to the words on the wall to help students remember word meanings, taking care to use songs that were played on their most-listened-to radio stations. For example, to help them remember the word melancholy, I attached it to the lyrics from Mary J. Blige's song "Be Happy": "All I really want is to be happy." The students retained *sad* as the definition of *melancholy*. Other vocabulary words were attached to songs the students' parents listened to. For example, the word *cease* was attached to Diana Ross's song "Stop! in the name of love." This approach, in addition to helping students improve vocabulary retention, also gave them a bit of music history—and it was fun. In this way, many of my students became excited about learning words. They also began to use the words in their writing. Introducing words that the students would come across in text significantly improved their sight and meaning vocabularies.

Semantic Mapping

Semantic mapping is a visual strategy for vocabulary expansion and extension of knowledge. It displays, in categories, how words are related to other words. Semantic mapping can prepare students to understand, assimilate, and evaluate new information. It helps them develop prior knowledge by seeing the relationships in a given topic. It also encourages students to become active learners.

The words I would ask students to map were always central to the text they were required to read. For example, during a lesson about anthrax that involved the use of text from a local newspaper, I asked students to map the word *warfare*, because the term *biological warfare* was central to the text. In semantic mapping, it is important that students not simply repeat

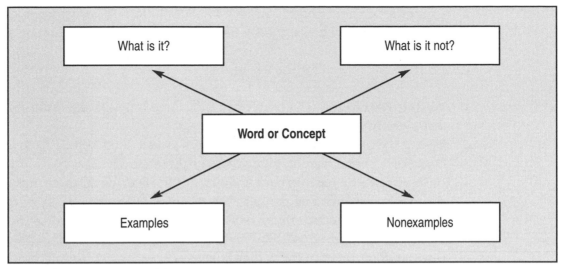

FIGURE 7.3 Generic Semantic Map

the definition of a word or concept having only a limited understanding of it. They should understand and be able to give examples of what the term means and what it does not (nonexamples). This provides them with the best opportunity for comprehending the term as it is used across multiple contexts. Figure 7.3 provides a template for a semantic map that can be adjusted to the purpose of the lesson.

NURTURING FLUENCY

Fluency, the ability to read text automatically, accurately, and with expression, is often neglected in reading instruction with adolescents. Nurturing reading fluency is important because there is a positive relationship between reading fluency and comprehension. Fluency allows students to connect the beginning of text to the middle of the text and on to the end of the text. The goal of nurturing students' fluency is to increase their reading speed and reduce the number of meaning-changing omissions, meaning-changing substitutions, and repeated words. As with the word-study activities described in the previous section, nurturing reading fluency should be integrated into the curriculum in meaningful ways, not be an end unto itself.

To nurture my students' reading fluency, I got them involved in fluency development lessons. Here's how such a lesson is conducted:

1. Choose a brief text (50–200 words). Provide copies for each student.
2. Do the lesson once a week. (Each lesson takes about 10 to 15 minutes.)

Here is the basic format for the lesson:

1. Read the text to the class (once, twice, or three times). Students listen and identify words they want repeated.
2. Discuss the content of the text and how it was read (loud, soft, fast, etc.).
3. Organize a choral reading (done twice or three times).
4. Have students divide into pairs and practice the text two or three times each with a partner. The partner gives positive feedback.
5. Have students choose one or two words from the text to go on the word wall.
6. Have students practice the text at home.
7. Assess students' oral reading fluency.

I assessed each student's fluency once a week at the beginning of the school year. I began by telling them that they had a perfect score (100 points) to begin with, and that the score was theirs to keep or lose. For each miscue—a repetition, a substitution, or an omission—four points would be deducted. If a student miscued on three words, for example, that student's fluency score would be 88 out of 100 points. Prior to my assessing them, the students participated in paired repeated readings and assessed each other (see Figure 7.4). The guidelines for the paired reading were as follows:

1. Each student is given a copy of the text.
2. While one partner reads the text aloud, the other listens attentively, helping with words *if asked to do so*.
3. The reader self-evaluates the first reading by considering such factors as speed, smoothness, expression, and attention to punctuation and circles the rating for Reading 1 on the evaluation sheet.
4. The reader rereads the passage, striving for improvement, and self-evaluates again.
5. The listener provides feedback on the form.
6. The two switch roles and repeat steps 2 through 5.
7. The teacher collects and reviews the evaluation sheets.

I made sure that the students were given texts at their grade level. I also wanted the texts to aid knowledge construction; although the main goal

PAIRED REPEATED READING EVALUATION

Reader _____ Date _____

Passage Used _____

How did I read: (circle one)

Reading 1: I read   great   well   so-so   not very well

Reading 2: I read   great   well   so-so   not very well

Reading 3: I read   great   well   so-so   not very well

What I did best in my reading:

Today I listened to _____ read.

Reading 2: Here's how my partner's reading got better (place an X on the appropriate line):

_____ My partner read more smoothly.

_____ My partner read with more expression.

_____ My partner knew more words.

_____ My partner stopped for punctuation.

Reading 3: Here's how my partner's reading got better:

_____ My partner read more smoothly.

_____ My partner read with more expression.

_____ My partner knew more words.

_____ My partner stopped for punctuation.

FIGURE 7.4 Paired Repeated Reading Evaluation

was to nurture fluency, I would select texts that enhanced the students' understanding of the lessons being discussed in class. The fluency development lessons also gave students the opportunity to connect with the word study activities. Some of the text selections I chose were the Declaration of Independence, the preamble to the U.S. Constitution, Martin Luther King's "I Have a Dream" speech, and Abraham Lincoln's Gettysburg Address. These texts are cognitively challenging and put students into contact with democratic principles. Other texts I chose led them to examine their rights to full participation as citizens of the United States.

Over the course of a school year, I found that the need for certain instructional approaches would shift. Students needed more time for word study and fluency development at the beginning of the year. As the year progressed, they needed to spend less time on decoding and fluency. This allowed us to give more time to vocabulary development and comprehension instruction.

IMPROVING COMPREHENSION

Students are better able to comprehend text when they receive explicit strategy instruction. This is particularly true of students who are unaware of what reading strategies to use and when to use them. Explicit strategy instruction also benefits students who must read increasingly complex material. Like the other subjects described in this chapter, reading strategies also should be taught in meaningful contexts. Unlike test practice materials or texts that help students "get and forget" the answers because the material does not relate to their lives, meaningful texts can both help them understand content across disciplines and enrich their lives. Students should receive instruction that equips them with pre-reading strategies (for example, previewing text, turning titles and subheadings into questions, establishing a purpose for reading), during-reading strategies (monitoring comprehension, creating visual images, constructing questions, confirming and disconfirming prior notions, rereading), and post-reading strategies (answering questions, extending the text, connecting their reading to writing). Students should also have reasons for wanting to comprehend the text to offset the "Why do we have to read this?" or "What does this have to do with me?" syndrome.

Teachers should have a clear sense of what they want to accomplish with the texts they select and a rationale for why their students should invest their time in the texts. The teaching skills and strategies used should enable students to comprehend the material independently and engage them in the active process of constructing meaning. Getting students to monitor their comprehension, employ self-questioning strategies, examine the relationship between questions and answers, and construct graphic organizers can be accomplished with text that increases their knowledge base.

Several approaches worked well with my students. To promote active engagement, I gave them explicit instruction in question-answer-evidence technique. I realized this was necessary when I found that students were attempting to answer comprehension questions by simply copying portions of the text that contained the same words as the questions. This was no good. I wanted students to demonstrate their competence; I was less interested in so-called correct responses. I therefore taught my students how to determine if their answers to comprehension questions were correct. I told them to keep the following points in mind when they answered questions:

1. Just because the text has the same words as the question does not mean the answer is correct.
2. The answer must fit the question—or, in other words, "If the answer does not fit, you must acquit." (Students were amused by this allusion to the O. J. Simpson murder trial.)
3. Analyze your answer carefully; look for a link that would make it false.

The following are some student responses to questions that became part of our lessons on question-answer-evidence technique, the idea being to find whether the evidence matched or did not match the answer given.

Q. The author believes that reading *Habits of Race in America* will cause dangerous social errors. (True or false?)
A. True.
E. "Reading this guide *will spare you* painful dangerous social errors."

The evidence proves that the answer "true" is wrong. Therefore, this is a question-answer-evidence *mismatch*.

Q. How has socially constructed behavior survived? (Short-answer question)
A. Because people are prejudiced.
E. A black family moving into a poor "white" area was attacked for "bringing down the neighborhood."

The evidence does not support the answer given; instead, it is just an example of prejudice. Therefore, this is a question-answer-evidence *mismatch*.

Q. Why is the voice of the poor often overlooked in political campaigns? (Multiple-choice question)
A. The poor do not finance political campaigns. (The wording of the choice provided)
E. "The poor contribute little money to political campaigns."

This is a question-answer-evidence *match*.

Having students cite evidence to prove their responses increases their engagement with the text. Comprehension-monitoring activities and graphic organizers also increase students' engagement with the text. Using embedded questions (Weir 1998) and cloze activities, I found, were also effective with my students.

Embedding questions directly into the text (see Figure 7.5 for an example) allowed me to steer students' attention to the important parts of the text. It also helped them focus their attention and encouraged

---

EXAMINING GEOMETRY ON ITS OWN TERMS

About ten years ago a fundamental riddle in my life was partly answered. I had been wondering why so many cultures, religious symbols, corporate logos, and kindergarten classrooms were full of the regular polygons, especially the 60-degree triangle, the square, the pentagon, the hexagon, and the octagon—and, though I did not include it in my musings at the time, the clock, or dodecagon. In classrooms, one finds them in the forms of blocks, pattern puzzles, the subject of countless coloring and cut-out exercises, and in the string constructs of geo-boards. These basic geometric shapes turn up everywhere. Language does not seem to matter. Culture does not seem to matter. They turn up on all continents, in many cultures, and occur with every civilization that has ever risen and passed away. (Why does the author believe that basic geometric shapes show up everywhere?) _____ (Think and search.)

When geometry is explored on its own terms, an extraordinary intellectual journey awaits. It begins with two points and is guided by a few self-evident rules and carried out by a cheap set of tools: a compass for making circles and arcs and a ruler for drawing lines. (What tools are needed to explore geometry?)_____ (Right there.)

Introduced to students as young as eight or eighty years, one soon finds that geometric designs are all mathematically logical. (What is suggested about geometric designs?) The geometry is a science, grounded by physical limitations, reducible to number, and pleasing to the eye. And while students drawing geometric designs think they're doing art, they will also be doing math and science. (How can art be used to support other content area subjects?) _____ (On your own.)

One of the direct benefits of learning geometry on its own terms is the impact it will have on art programs. Art programs are continuously under fire from local and national quarters that threaten their already weakened budgets. If geometry could be reconnected with art in national curricula, we could break through the ideological straitjacket that forces us to teach science and art as opposites. It would provide a direct and concrete bridge that ties them together. (How can the focus on high science standards at local, state, and national levels be used to argue for funding for art programs?) _____

_____

_____

FIGURE 7.5 Embedded Questions

CLOZE ACTIVITY

When West African tribes were brought to the New World in chains, they carried their music and traditions with them. The powerful rhythms of African percussion influenced American music. Slave work songs were created in the African tradition of call-and-response. To tell a _____, a song leader would call out a line and the _____ would respond to the call. Many slaveholders did not allow the slaves to _____ to each other, so the only way they could _____ was through song. They developed many _____ ways of getting their secret messages across in the _____. Slaves also sang soulful songs called "spirituals" to express their _____ beliefs, feelings, and desire for _____. Spirituals and work songs are part of the foundation of the American _____ form known as jazz. Also, in the early 1890s the blues _____ from these traditions. In performing the blues, singers used the power of their _____ to express their feelings.

FIGURE 7.6 Cloze Activity

comprehension monitoring. I wanted my students to assess their understanding at different points throughout their reading of the text.

This embedded-question activity makes students think about question-and-answer relationships (Raphael 1986). It also teaches them to construct questions as they read—in effect, embedding their own questions into the text.

Cloze activities also encouraged my students to monitor their comprehension and helped them use multiple cueing systems to construct a text that makes sense. (Figure 7.6 is a sample cloze activity.)

Other comprehension strategies can be taught to students in response to identified needs. The goal is to integrate word study and vocabulary development, fluency development, and comprehension instruction in meaningful ways so that they are not viewed as disparate activities.

As mentioned earlier, there is nothing magical about the instructional approaches I used with my students. What made them effective, I believe, were the following features: the approaches were used consistently; they were embedded into meaningful contexts; they gave me opportunities to give immediate and corrective feedback; and they were planned in response to my students' strengths and weaknesses. These instructional approaches were also informed by research indicating that students need instructional activities with multiple components. Like Socrates in the epigraph to this chapter, I tried to make every instructional step in my framework for teaching reading go in the direction of helping my young travelers find their way through text.

CHAPTER 8

DISCUSSING
TEXTS

Lying on my cot, I think about everything that has happened over the last year. There was nothing extraordinary in my life. No bolt of lightning came out of the sky. I didn't say a magical word and turn into somebody different. But here I am, maybe on the verge of losing my life, or the life I used to have.

Walter Dean Myers, *Monster*

I can't remember when I decided I wanted to be an intellectual. I am not even sure if that's the sort of thing one fully determines before it happens. For that matter, I can't remember when I became an intellectual, a person with a great passion to think and study and to distribute the fruits of his labor in useful form. There was no bolt of lightning for me; unlike St. Paul, I didn't have a dramatic conversion that saved me from ignorance and put me on the path of learning.

Michael Eric Dyson, *The Michael Eric Dyson Reader*

In Chapter 4, I mentioned that black male students' relationships with texts need to be discussed as part of their literacy learning. In the epigraphs above, two black males have taken divergent paths in their lives. In both cases, however, they refer to a "bolt of lightning." In the first quote, Walter Dean Myers's fictional black male teenager is sitting in a prison cell, accused of murder, trying to figure out how he managed to put himself so close to death at such a young age. There was nothing extraordinary about his life, he says—no "bolt of lightning." In the second quote, Professor Michael Eric Dyson has been asked about his development as a scholar as he is being interviewed at the University of North Carolina. He too says he cannot recall a specific turning point in his life, a dramatic conversion that saved him from ignorance; there was no "bolt of lightning" for this professor who had his beginnings in an urban ghetto. Both of these males had similar upbringings, but starkly different outcomes; neither can explain why or how.

Both quotes get to the core of what it means to be a black man in America. A pendulum swings both ways for them. On one side are hopes and dreams, where potential can lead to promise. On the other is defeat, where hopes unfulfilled become a record of human tragedy. It is difficult to determine from simply reading the two epigraphs which one is from a fictional source and which is from nonfiction. Oftentimes fiction mirrors reality and reality mirrors fiction. Both can be used in powerful ways to help black males craft a unique place for themselves. Their teachers' contribution, however, will be limited if they focus only on the cognitive dimensions of literacy learning described in Chapter 7. Teachers must also discuss texts with their black male students in responsive ways, in order to help them land on the side of the pendulum that swings toward promise and possibility. Discussing texts with these young men should help them extend the ideas contained in the texts into their own lives and make connections to their own experiences.

Text discussions, in short, should help students create meaning. This is what the teacher in Tobias Wolff's text was trying to do when he asked his students to examine what it means to be a son, as described in Chapter 4, and it is what I was trying to do with the young man who was recently released from prison, when I asked him to consider Rifkin's *The End of Work* and Galbraith's *The Good Society.* Text discussions should go beyond answering comprehension questions. They should move us to examine how we might apply new understandings from the text to our own existence and our own future. Discussing text with students requires that teachers understand that the meaning is not in the text per se, but is to be found in the text and the experiences the reader brings to it.

A teacher can discuss the two quotes at the beginning of this chapter in different ways depending on the students. For students who are ready to surrender their life chances before they can even formulate their life choices, the teacher can use the text of the young man lying on the cot to have the students examine their own life positions and how they are reacting to them. The second text can then be introduced to help the students understand that the idea of a bolt of lightning, or lack of one, works two ways. The absence of a bolt of lightning can become a metaphor that can be applied to other texts and contexts, not something to be understood for the moment of discussion of this text only, but extended into the students' own lives.

National achievement data suggest that texts are not being discussed effectively with adolescent students. In 1998, for example, only 33 percent of eighth-grade students and 40 percent of twelfth-grade students were reading at or above the proficient level. A large percentage of students are unable to extend the ideas of a text, make inferences, draw conclusions, and connect text to their own experiences. These ideas are contained in the definitions of "proficient" and "advanced" readers in grade 8 and grade 12 by the National Assessments of Educational Progress:

■ Proficient Grade 8: Eighth-grade students performing at the proficient level should be able to show an overall understanding of the text, including inferential as well as literal information. When reading text appropriate to eighth grade they should be able to extend the ideas in the text by making clear inferences from it, drawing conclusions, and making connections to their own experiences—including other reading experiences.

■ Advanced Grade 8: Eighth-grade students performing at the advanced level should be able to describe the more abstract themes and ideas in the overall text. When reading text appropriate to the eighth grade, they should be able to analyze both meaning and form and support their analyses explicitly with examples from the text; they should be able to extend information by relating it to their experiences and to world events. At this level, student responses should be thorough, thoughtful, and extensive.

■ Proficient Grade 12: Twelfth-grade students performing at the proficient level should be able to show an overall understanding of the text that includes inferential as well as literal information. When reading text appropriate to twelfth grade, they should be able to extend ideas by making inferences, drawing conclusions, and making connections to their own personal experiences and other readings. Connections between inference and text should be clear, even when implicit.

■ Advanced Grade 12: Twelfth-grade students performing at the advanced level should be able to describe more abstract themes and ideas in the overall text. When reading text appropriate to the twelfth grade, they should be able to analyze both the meaning and the form of the text and explicitly support their analyses with specific examples from the text. They should be able to extend the information from the text by relating it to their experiences and to the world.

Achievement gap data indicate that a large percentage of black males are failing to meet NAEP criteria for reading at the proficient and advanced levels. This is why I believe we need to strengthen text discussions with our black adolescent male students. Statistics from the U.S. Department of Justice tell us that a high percentage of black males are arrested or incarcerated. This is why I believe we need to strengthen text discussions with our black adolescent male students. Data from the U.S. Department of Labor indicate that a high percentage of black males are unemployed. This is why I believe we need to strengthen text discussions with our black adolescent male students. Data from the U.S. Department of Education indicate that college enrollment is declining for black males. This is why I believe we need to strengthen text discussions with our black adolescent male students.

To improve text discussions and, by doing so, ultimately address some of the issues described above requires that teachers attend to the strands of learning described in the previous chapters. That is:

■ Discussing texts with black males cannot be separated from the role of literacy instruction, the importance of curriculum orientation, and the need for a culturally responsive approach to literacy teaching.

■ Discussing texts with these—or any—students is not possible if they do not have the skills and strategies that anchor a comprehensive approach to literacy teaching.

■ Discussing texts with black male students cannot be done effectively without an awareness of their identity and their definition of masculinity, as pointed out in the research on boys and reading.

■ Discussing texts with black male students cannot be separated from the turmoil they are forced to endure.

These issues should frame teachers' thinking as they plan text discussions.

PROMPTING MEANINGFUL RESPONSES

Getting students to offer genuine responses, and not allowing them to search for and parrot the teacher's interpretation of a text should be at the core of discussing texts with black male students. Teachers must create a culture that honors students' voices in the interpretation of texts. Teresa Herbert (1995) notes, "If we provide quality literature (a problem when limited to an older textbook) and allow students to respond from authentic voices (not necessarily answering the teacher's questions), then we are doing more to help students respond authentically" (p. 54). She adds that "literature's vast potential to awaken humans to that which is beautiful in life should not be undermined by teachers who require students to interpret literature in a way they perceive to be right" (p. 60). In her attempt to use a response-centered approach to nurture students' voices in the interpretation of text, she learned several lessons that may be valuable for nurturing text discussions with adolescents:

- Use small groups and have students share their reflections with each other.
- Continue to reflect and refine approaches to get students to engage with text.
- Allow time—weeks, perhaps even months—for students to become "real responders" to text.
- Model the types of response you expect from students.
- Respect students as competent readers, writers, learners, and human beings.

RESPECTING STUDENTS' RESPONSES

Herbert (1995) also points out that discussing texts effectively with adolescent students requires some risk-taking. Students who are not used to providing authentic responses to texts will resist doing so until they begin to trust that their responses will be valued and respected. Teachers who are used to having students interpret texts one way can become intimidated when students start to respond to texts in authentic ways. Student responses that take issue with the text or that disagree with the teacher's interpretation may be viewed as a threat to a teacher's authority. I recall being challenged by students during a discussion of history texts. Many of my black students did not want to discuss slavery, although I believed it was important subject matter for them to learn. It was also a required topic in social studies. The students felt as though I was forcing them to accept a past of victimization. As their teacher, I could not simply dismiss their concerns and tell them they would learn about slavery because I said they needed to learn about it. I had to respect their concerns and negotiate. This led to our discussing the notion that vestiges of slavery could be found in the students' own lives in the present—in various community and health practices, in the educational system, in the economic impoverishment of their households, and in the modern-day shackles that do not bind the hands, but the minds. The discussion of slavery was made possible by my introduction of alternative texts, such as the Willie Lynch letter described in Chapter 5.

My students' refusal to discuss certain culturally specific text topics is not unique. Jennifer Obidah (1998), in her chapter describing ways to engage black high school students in text discussions, writes:

> *Educators and parents are painfully aware that many Black students are traumatized and humiliated when reading about slavery and other topics concerning their ancestry. They often report that Black students do not want to discuss slavery or be identified with Africa (King and Mitchell 1990), and many admit they lack the conceptual tools to intervene in this dangerous dynamic (Hawkins 1990).*

She explains how well-intentioned teachers may find it difficult to engage some students with texts even after introducing culturally inclusive texts. Obidah found that the solution to engaging her black students with text was paying attention to the literate currency adolescents use to construct, read, and reproduce text. "Literate currency" refers to the bodies of knowledge in general use among groups of people. Obidah notes that peer literacy, school literacy, home/community literacy, and popular culture literacy are but a few examples of the many sources of information adolescents utilize at any given time to make sense of the world in which they live. She writes, "When teachers make spaces for dialogue that include students' literate currency, it begins a reciprocal process of learning between them and their students, with an end product of higher levels of student engagement, interest, and desire to acquire new knowledge as its benefits to their lives are made clear" (p. 56). Regarding black students' literate currency, she recommends the following:

- Develop counterknowledge to supplement incomplete or biased curricular texts.
- Challenge the knowledge in the textbooks—even so-called multicultural textbooks—and allow students to do the same.
- Pay attention to students' uninterested responses to teaching and learning processes.
- Facilitate space for students to make new images of themselves; do not impose an identity on them.
- Make students' literate currency salient in the classroom.

TEACHER DISPOSITION

Discussing texts with black males involves more than just opening space for them to talk about their reading. I have found that the teacher's disposition toward the text and his or her attitude about its significance matter greatly. I recall an incident during my second year of teaching. My students were reading Mildred Taylor's (1976) *Roll of Thunder, Hear My Cry*. We were discussing two major themes in the book: home ownership and living debt-free. These were characteristics of the Logan family that gave them power in the segregated, racist southern town where they lived. At the time, I was in debt and living in my mother's home. I felt like a fraud when one student asked me if I owned my own property. When I told the class I lived with my mother, they laughed. They did not understand why a teacher—a professional—did not own property. It was at this point that Taylor's book became more than a novel; it became a seed of empowerment. Our conversation moved away from a banal discussion of the text toward our beliefs about how one should live. By the end of the school year, I was able to invite my students to my new home and discuss the process of buying a house.

Jeffrey Wilhelm (1997), in his description of ten responses that students use as they create, experience, and respond to literary texts, asserts that there are both connective and reflective responses to text. Reading Taylor's novel was no longer a cognitive exercise for me and my students; it was a way of becoming. The literature was connected to our lives in the classroom; we were able to recognize the significance of this work of historical fiction. We then used this historical fiction as a bridge to discuss economics and home ownership. This experience made me realize that discussions of text have to be authentic for teachers as well as students.

CONSIDERING TURMOIL

For text discussions with black males to be effective, teachers must take into account the turmoil in their students' lives. Ideally, the texts that are selected should have multiple functions. For each text being considered, ask the following questions:

1. Can the text be used to strengthen black male identity?
2. Will the text challenge them cognitively?
3. Will it move them to examine their in-school and out-of-school lives?
4. Will it give them the opportunity to practice the reading strategies needed to comprehend text independently?

In addition, the texts need to be discussed in culturally responsive ways.

The way literature is discussed in the class profoundly affects black males' engagement or disengagement as readers. Literature should help these young men understand history, substantiate their existence, and give them a chance to critically examine possible political, social, and cultural undertakings that may present themselves in the future.

Consider my class's engagement with two texts: James Baldwin's *My Dungeon Shook: Letter to My Nephew on the One Hundredth Anniversary of the Emancipation* and Richard Wright's *Black Boy: A Record of Childhood and Youth.* I selected the texts because they perform the multiple functions described above. In addition, they connect well with the conceptual strands described in Chapter 7. I also considered the length of the texts. Both are relatively short texts that can be reread and reexamined as discussions take place; and they can be completed in one sitting, which can give students a feeling of accomplishment.

Baldwin's essay can inspire comparison of black men's situation at the time the text was written over forty years ago and their situation today. It can be used to help black male students critique society and examine their place within in it. Baldwin provides rich kernels of wisdom that can be openly explored. For example:

> *He was defeated long before he died because at the bottom of his heart, he really believed what white people said about him. (p. 3)*

> *You can only be destroyed by believing that you really are what the white world calls a nigger. (p. 4)*

But it is not possible that the authors of devastation should be innocent. (p. 5)

This innocent country set you down in a ghetto in which, in fact, it intended that you should perish. (p. 6)

You were born where you were born and faced the future that you faced because you were black and for no other reason. The limits of your ambition were, thus, expected to be set forever. (p. 7)

You were not expected to aspire to excellence; you were expected to make peace with mediocrity. (p. 7)

Know whence you came. If you know whence you came, there is really no limit of where you can go. (p. 7)

Well the black man has functioned in the white man's world as a fixed star, as an immovable pillar. (p. 8)

You, don't be afraid. I said that it was intended that you should perish in the ghetto, perish by never being allowed to go behind the white man's definitions, by never being allowed to spell your proper name. (p. 9)

For this is your home, my friend, do not be driven from it; great men have done great things here, and will again, and we can make America what America must become. (p. 9)

The very time I thought I was lost, My dungeon shook and my chains fell off. (p. 9)

The key to discussing this text with your black male students is to help them make connections between a text written more than forty years ago and contemporary circumstances. For example, you might ask them to look for the advice Baldwin is giving his nephew. After identifying that advice, they can discuss whether the advice is relevant or irrelevant in today's society. In other words, if Baldwin wrote the letter today, what would he need to change? To help them begin, you might consider creating a chart like the one shown in Figure 8.1 for the students to complete.

Prior to reading the text the students could be told to consider the following:

1. What part(s) of the letter stands out to you the most and why?

BALDWIN CHART	
Original Message	**The Message if Written Today** (Would it be the same or different? If different, rewrite the message as you think it would appear today.)
You were not expected to aspire to excellence; you were expected to make peace with *mediocrity*.	

FIGURE 8.1 Baldwin Chart

2. How is this essay relevant for young black men growing up in today's society? How is it relevant to *all* young men growing up in today's society?

3. What does this letter suggest about the connection between the black male's destiny and America's destiny?

To move black males away from accepting a victim's mentality, we need to help them realize that they are responsible for determining their life's outcomes. As they critique society, they must critique their place within that society. At the center of the critique, they need to consider whether they are accomplices to their shortcomings or failures. They need to examine their actions—or inactions—both inside and outside of school. They need to think about whether there is a "major conspiracy" that is preventing them from doing well in school. Is there a major conspiracy that keeps them from coming into contact with meaningful print? Is *mediocrity* (word on the word wall) acceptable or unacceptable? Encourage them to examine their role in their own "dungeon construction." In the process, they can also examine the teacher's role, the school's role, and the community's role in "dungeon construction." They can examine their placement in low-level reading tracks; they can examine their position in low-achieving schools. Honest dialogue should be encouraged.

MAKING CONNECTIONS

Discussing texts is made more powerful when the text is connected to the students' lives and to other texts. I used Baldwin's idea of shaking dungeons as a lead into Wright's *Black Boy: A Record of Childhood and Youth.* In this autobiographical account, Wright explains how, instead of succumbing to the idleness he experienced in school, he decided to write a story. Writing created a tension he did not anticipate. Other students doubted his desire to write, as illustrated in the dialogue below:

"Did you really write that story?"
"Yes."
"Why?"
"Because I wanted to."
"Where did you get it from?"
"I made it up."
"You didn't. You copied it out of a book."
"If I had, no one would publish it."
"But what are they publishing it for?"
"So people can read it."
"Who told you to do that?"
"Nobody."
"Then why did you do it?"
"Because I wanted to," I said again. (pp. 196–197)

In addition, Wright was criticized by his grandmother, who referred to his fictional story as the "devil's work"; his mother discouraged him from writing so that others would not view him as being "weak-minded"; and his uncle told young Wright that his story had no point. Wright eventually came to feel as though he had committed a crime.

I suggested to my students that Wright was surrounded by "dungeon makers" and that these "dungeon makers" came in all shapes and sizes. I then asked the class to examine how Wright resisted his dungeons and what implications his actions held for them.

With guidance and support from each other, the students came up with many insights about this text. For example, they identified that Wright built up a dream within himself. This is reflected in the quotation "I was building up in me a dream which the entire educational system of the South had been rigged to stifle" (p. 199). They also discerned that Wright shaped a yearning in himself. This is reflected in the quote "In me was shaping a yearning for a kind of consciousness, a mode of being that the way of life about me had said could not be, must not be, and upon which the penalty of death had been placed" (p. 200).

Wright makes the point that one cannot be limited by either the views of others or one's present condition. By extension, he is also saying that one may attend an impoverished school with impoverished thinkers, but that is not the student's problem, it is the school's problem. Students may have to deal with people who do not understand or care to understand their ambitions. Again, that's not the student's problem, but the problem of others. They may have to fight to push their way upstream, but going upstream is worth it if they win what awaits them at the end. With the help of Wright, my students came to understand that they need a new kind of consciousness in order to shake their dungeons.

I connected Baldwin's and Wright's texts to shore up resistance in my black male students. I encouraged them to examine the currents in their society that they had to push against. I encouraged them to identify their "dungeon makers." I asked them to map out a strategy and describe how they planned to execute that strategy inside and outside of school. I encouraged them to resist, resist, resist the turmoil in their lives.

Here are several other short pieces that I have found to be effective with the young men I taught; all are in an anthology of African American Literature (1998):

"Narrative of the Life of Frederick Douglass" by Frederick Douglass
"Letter to Thomas Jefferson" by Benjamin Banneker
"Booker T. and W. E. B." by Dudley Randall
"Crusade for Justice" by Ida B. Wells
"If We Must Die" by Claude McKay
"America" by Claude McKay
"Mother to Son" by Langston Hughes
"A Black Man Talks of Reaping" by Arna Bontemps
"Lineage" by Margaret Walker
"The Man Who Was Almost a Man" by Richard Wright
"The Kind of Light That Shines in Texas" by Reginald McKnight
"Malcolm X" from *The Autobiography of Malcolm X* by Alex Haley and
    Malcolm X
"SOS" by Amiri Baraka

There is no simple formula for discussing texts with black male students. The discussions evolve from specific contexts. One of the goals of text discussion is to get students to experience the richness of the text in their teacher's presence. If we as teachers discuss texts effectively, we too will be transformed as we discover new meanings, share our beliefs and experiences, and help our students shape themselves as we too are being shaped.

CHAPTER 9

STRENGTHENING THE ASSESSMENT PROFILE

Today, more than ever, the traditional boundaries between politics, culture, technology, finance, national security, and ecology are disappearing. You often cannot explain one without referring to the others, and you cannot explain the whole without reference to them all. Therefore, to be an effective foreign affairs analyst or reporter, you have to learn how to arbitrage information from disparate perspectives and then weave it all together to produce a picture of the world you would never have if you looked at it from one perspective.

Thomas Friedman, *The Lexus and the Olive Tree*

The epigraph of this chapter is taken from Thomas Friedman's national best seller *The Lexus and the Olive Tree*. In it, Friedman emphasizes the need to gather information from multiple perspectives and weave them together to produce a picture of the world that is not possible from only one perspective. Later in the book, he discusses the need to look at the world in multiple dimensions, to systematically connect the dots and make order from chaos. This allows one to study the relationship among existing variables that can potentially influence outcomes. He notes, "With a complex nonlinear system you have to break it up into pieces and then study each aspect, and then study the strong interaction between them all. Only this way can you describe the whole system" (p. 28). Friedman's words are particularly salient when teachers assess the literacy needs of their black male students who are experiencing turmoil. Earlier I described how one must take a complete audit of the turmoil in these young men's lives in order to provide them with effective literacy instruction.

Teachers have to be prepared to assess several dimensions of the reader and his reading. Taking too limited a view can result in instructional practices, although research based, being misapplied and students' performance on reading-related tasks misinterpreted. Two recent experiences of mine come to mind.

For the past two years, I have suffered from daily, recurring headaches. To assess the problem, I initially visited my primary care physician, who recommended that I keep a "headache log" for two weeks and sent me home with some extra-strength Tylenol. The pills gave me temporary relief, but the headaches continued. Next, the doctor recommended a CAT scan. This identified a sinus problem, and sinus medication was prescribed. Again, I received some temporary relief, but the headaches continued. I was then sent to an ear, nose, and throat specialist, who checked for allergies. The specialist told me that strong smells, such as smoke and cologne, and eating chocolate were causing my headaches, and prescribed three sprays and pills to be taken daily. I received temporary relief again; but again, the headaches continued. Some time later, one of my wisdom teeth was causing me pain. I went to the dentist, who identified that my wisdom tooth and an upper molar needed to be removed. The upper molar, the dentist said, was pressing against my sinus nerve. I had dental surgery. Days after the surgery, I experienced a full day without a headache after more than two years.

Each of my doctors used research-based tools or made research-based recommendations to cure my headache. Each, however, with the exception of the dentist, was limited by the tools he used. They could not, or did not, use multiple forms of assessment to solve the problem. As a result, I only received temporary relief because the doctors were unable to identify the root cause of the problem. As Friedman might put it, a single perspective is overly limiting and often flawed.

I recall another experience I had, this one while I was a reading specialist supporting teachers in grades 4–8. One of the teachers repeatedly complained to me about her students' decoding ability. She explained that her sixth-grade students had comprehension problems because they lacked phonics skills. I proceeded to visit her classroom and observe several lessons over several days. I noticed that students were having difficulty with some of the multisyllable words in the texts they were required to read. I also noticed that the moment a student hesitated when reading orally, the teacher or another student would say the word without giving the reader the chance to decode the word independently. This prevented me from assessing the students' decoding strengths and weaknesses as they read.

I decided to use leveled word lists from a qualitative reading inventory in order to help me assess the students' ability to decode words automatically and compare that to their ability to decode words when they were given time to analyze the words. The results I gathered from the qualitative reading inventory indicated that, on average, the students were able to identify words at greater than 90 percent accuracy when they were given time to analyze the words. When the words were flashed for only one second, however, the students, on average, were able to decode only 70 percent of the words at their grade level.

These findings suggested to me that the students' problems with comprehension were more related to fluency than decoding. I shared my analysis with the teacher and the students. We then agreed to establish a classroom climate that provided all students more time to decode words that they did not immediately recognize—no longer would others blurt out the words. We also planned fluency and word study instruction (such as decoding by analogy) using text that the students were required to read in order to respond to students' needs at the word level. The goal was to contextualize the word study instruction and not teach words in isolation. The answer to these students' difficulties at the word level did not require more phonics instruction; instead, they needed word study instruction that would help them quickly recognize phonogram patterns in multisyllable words. Without a careful and thorough assessment profile of students' decoding abilities, this teacher might have given her students more phonics instruction, which would have resulted in misdirected energy and effort.

GETTING A COMPLETE PICTURE

How does one develop a comprehensive assessment profile that can be useful for addressing the literacy needs of adolescents?

Teachers must come to know individual students through watching them, listening to them, and interacting with them using meaningful literacy activities (Ivey 1999). To ensure that students get the specific help they need requires that their teacher have a comprehensive picture of their strengths and weaknesses. The assessment plan should consider the student's cognitive dimensions of literacy (for example, comprehension, word knowledge) as well as the affective dimensions (such as the types of materials the student values, attitude toward reading). Identifying students' literacy-related strengths and weakness requires an assessment approach that is ongoing, involves both formal and informal techniques, and extends across several areas of reading. The teacher's assessment practices have to be wide enough and frequent enough in order to provide effective, responsive instruction. Too often, assessment practices have been used to highlight the deficits of black males. It is more important for teachers to use assessment practices to improve their practice and to avoid marginalizing these students' chances and choices.

In the previous chapter, I discussed the need to choose literacy instruction, curriculum orientations, and forms of pedagogy most suitable for developing the literacy of black males. In addition, a profile of students' word knowledge, comprehension, fluency, and writing is required for teachers to plan responsive instruction. It is insufficient to say that students have problems with reading comprehension without being able to describe exactly what that means.

Several years ago one of my colleagues informed a parent that her son had a reading problem. The mother asked the teacher how she might best help her son at home. The teacher replied that the youngster simply needed to read more. The mother persisted: "Are there certain things I should help him with?" The teacher responded, "Just have him read more and he should be okay." Then the mother asked the teacher to suggest some readings for her son. The teacher responded, "It does not matter what he reads as long as he is reading."

This exchange I find disturbing on several levels. First, the teacher did not have a sense of what was causing the young man's difficulty with reading. Just saying that a student has a "reading problem" is too open-ended.

Second, the teacher did not give the mother specific suggestions on how to support her son at home and help him improve his reading. For example, if the problem was one of comprehension, the teacher could have recommended the following:

- Support the young man's reading of multisyllable words because he was having difficulty with them, and this was slowing him down.
- Help him pay close attention to the meaning of the text as he goes from paragraph to paragraph because he has not been monitoring his comprehension.
- Help him set a purpose for his reading by turning headings and sub-headings into questions.
- Have him form visual representations of what is occurring in the text, perhaps by having him draw a picture to demonstrate his understanding of the text.
- Encourage him to complete graphic organizers (for example, a semantic map or a compare-contrast chart) while reading to incite more active engagement with text. (The teacher can then give some forms for the graphic organizers to the parent.)

Of course, these suggestions may not pertain to the needs of this particular student; they are simply examples of specific recommendations that can be offered by a teacher who has insight into a student's difficulty comprehending text.

A third problem with this exchange is that the teacher told the mother that "it does not matter" what her son reads "as long as he is reading." This communicates the message that text does not matter and the young man's interests do not matter. It is quite possible that as a result of this conference this parent will go home and say to her son, "Sit down and read something! That is why you have a reading problem now—you don't read enough." This will do little to motivate a struggling reader who has difficulty handling text, or a student who is not interested in reading. I can imagine this young man responding to the mother's exhortation by resisting reading, pretending to read, or reading without caring about what he is reading, instead of engaging with text in a way that would allow him to practice strategies independently, and becoming smarter because of his reading.

CLOSE-UPS

To develop useful, complete profiles of their students, teachers need to obtain a variety of close-ups: cognitive close-ups, pedagogical close-ups, psychological close-ups, and in some cases physiological close-ups. These details will help teachers make specific recommendations, like those mentioned above, and plan effective, targeted instruction.

Cognitive Close-Ups

Cognitive close-ups include the following:

- A profile of the student's strengths and weaknesses at the word level:
  Is the student having difficulty decoding?
  Is the student having difficulty decoding words quickly?
  Does the student have a limited vocabulary?
- A profile at the text level:
  Does the student monitor his comprehension?
  Does the student make meaning-changing miscues?
  Does the student lack reading fluency?
  Does the student attempt to use the same strategies for all text?
- Notes on difficulties at the conceptual level:
  Does the student have a strong concept of reading?
  Does the student have a hard time figuring out why he cannot comprehend the text?

Pedagogical Close-Ups

Pedagogical close-ups include the following:

- A profile of instructional time:
  Is the student receiving explicit strategy instruction?
  Is a comprehensive framework of literacy instruction present?
  Is there more teacher talk than reading?
  How much class time does the student actually spend reading?
  Does the student have choice during instructional time?
  Is the student receiving instruction in a caring and supportive environment?
  Does the student have the opportunity to fail and recover?
  Is the student's culture considered during instruction and instructional planning?
  Is the student's identity as an adolescent considered during instruction and instructional planning?
- A profile of curriculum orientations:
  Is the student able to identify the relevance in the curriculum?

Is the curriculum decontextualized from the student's life?

Is the curriculum cognitively challenging?

Is the student's identity being developed within the curriculum framework?

Is the curriculum interesting?

- A profile of assessments:

Are there formal and informal assessments?

Are the assessments used to plan instruction?

Are a variety of assessments used? Is the student asked to do self-assessments?

Are the assessment results reported to the student in a way that can lead to improvement?

Do the assessments encourage or discourage participation?

Are the student's interests identified?

Psychological Close-Ups

Psychological close-ups include consideration of the following:

- Self-efficacy:
  Does the student attribute difficulties to ability or effort?
- Failure prevention:
  Is the student's goal to pass, not necessarily to learn?
- Emotional overload:
  Does the student feel stupid?
  Does the student experience frustration in class?
  Does the student suffer from a fear of embarrassment?

Physiological Close-Ups

Physiological close-ups may require the evaluation of an expert outside of the classroom to determine whether the student has any of the following:

- Difficulty retaining information.
- A specific medical condition.
- Vision problems.

I have found these assessment close-ups extremely useful as I have worked with students over the years. Building some of these considerations into my assessment plan has led me to do several things:

1. Plan assessments that incorporate the various components of the comprehensive framework of literacy teaching described in earlier chapters (word study and vocabulary development, comprehension, fluency and writing).
2. Survey students to determine what types of reading materials they prefer.
3. Monitor students' responses more carefully to determine aspects of the instruction they respond to best.
4. Use a variety of assessments.
5. Assess my methods if a high percentage of the students do not comprehend what I am trying to teach.
6. Invite students' voices into the assessment process every five weeks. I ask them five questions:
   What instructional approaches are working for you?
   What instructional approaches are not working for you?
   What should I continue doing as a teacher to help you become a better reader and writer?
   What should I change?
   What is my overall grade?

APPROACHES TO CHOOSE FROM

Figure 9.1 presents a summary of assessment approaches I used with my students that allowed me to identify their strengths and weaknesses and identify the instructional approaches and strategies that would be best for advancing their literacies. Of these approaches, the ones I found most useful were those that required students to cite evidence for all of the comprehension responses and those that enabled me to analyze the students' miscues. Requiring students to cite evidence, I found, increased their engagement with text, while analyzing miscues gave me a more complete picture of individual students' strengths at both the word level and the text level. The appendix contains examples of two assessments I used with my students to gather information about their awareness of strategies, their vocabulary, and their ability to answer different types of questions. Figure 9.2 provides some examples of how to analyze students' miscues.

The research on adolescent literacy suggests that there are some general guidelines for establishing a reciprocal relationship between teacher and student that can lead to effective and meaningful assessment practices:

ASSESSMENT APPROACHES

Type of approach	Reason for using	Type of text	How often?
Running records	Identify useful/problem strategies with words/text	Fiction, nonfiction	As needed
Cloze procedure	To determine whether students are monitoring their comprehension	Fiction, nonfiction	Weekly
Timed readings	To assess reading fluency	Fiction, nonfiction	Weekly
Character perspective chart	To assess students' understanding about major characters in a text	Fiction	As needed
One-pagers	Low-risk assessment that allows students to focus on parts of the text they find meaningful	Fiction, nonfiction	As needed
Decoding/vocabulary assessments	To assess students' decoding and vocabulary growth	Fiction, nonfiction	Daily
Observations	Identify ways to better address students' needs by paying attention to factors that may impede literacy development		Daily
Conferences	To allow students' voices into the assessment process and to make plans for improvement		Bimonthly
Student reflections and invited feedback	To allow students' voices into the assessment process		Five-week intervals

FIGURE 9.1 Assessment Approaches

1. Let students know ahead of time what will be expected.
2. Minimize risk by giving students time to prepare responses.
3. Strike a favorable balance between success and failure.
4. Provide clear indications about correctness.
5. Rehearse correct information by both speaking and highlighting it.
6. Avoid alienating students.

ANALYZING MISCUES

Visual Cues
The following are examples of a student's using visual cues while reading.

Text	Student	Explanation
I was playing with the /harmonica/.	I was playing with the /harmony/.	There is a small visual difference between /harmonica/ and /harmony/. When observing the miscue, the student read the beginning and the middle of the word correctly. The student attempted to read this word by relying on his or her ability to recognize word parts and putting those parts together to decode the word.
He wanted to /winterize/ the car.	He wanted to /winter/ the car.	There is a small visual difference between /winterize/ and /winter/. The student is probably more familiar with the concept of *winter* than *winterize*, and based on this prior knowledge makes a miscue that can be attributed to a reliance on processing the text visually.
The researcher was /vehement/ about finding the results.	The researcher was /vement/ about finding the results.	There is a small visual difference between /vehement/ and /vement/. The student read the beginning of the word and the end of the word correctly. It is probably the case that *vehement* is not one of the student's sight words. The student relies on phonetic skills in an attempt to decode the word.

Structural Cues
The following are examples of a student's using structural cues while reading.

Text	Student	Explanation
The politicians made a /pact/.	The politicians made a /part/.	The reader may know that people can make *parts*, and not be familiar with the word *pact*. This reader is probably relying on the structure of the text when making this miscue.
From under the animal's body, the /shield/ was removed.	From under the animal's body, the /shell/ was removed.	According to conventions of language, the word *shell* could be an appropriate substitution. This student has not decoded the end of the word and the middle of the word correctly. He or she was probably paying more attention to structural cues (syntax) than visual cues.
He had the /entry/ code.	He had the /entire/ code.	Again, the miscue *entire* fits all the conventions of language. This student probably relied on the structure of the text when making this miscue.

FIGURE 9.2 Analyzing Miscues

ANALYZING MISCUES

Meaning Cues
The following are examples of a student's using meaning cues while reading.

Text	Student	Explanation
His /father/ was not ready.	His /dad/ was not ready.	The meaning of the sentence is not altered. The student is constructing meaning while reading.
His parents told him to /clean/ his room.	His parents told him to /clean up/ his room.	The reader inserts the word *up* in the sentence. This is a meaning miscue. In terms of meaning, there is no difference between *clean* the room and *clean up* the room.

Questions to Ask
Look for patterns when analyzing miscues.
Interpret useful or problem strategies with words or texts:

- Is the reader monitoring comprehension?
- Are there multiple meaning-changing miscues?
- What is the rate of self-correction?
- Does the student have a poor concept of reading?
- How many cueing systems does the student use?
- What does the analysis reveal about substitutions, repetitions, and omissions?
- What pattern(s) do you notice at the word level?
- What pattern(s) do you notice at the text level?

FIGURE 9.2 Analyzing Miscues *(continued)*

7. Require participation, but avoid putting students on the spot.
8. Establish trust.
9. Engage students in conversations on how their actions affect their literacy development.
10. Involve students in the assessment process.
11. Use a variety of assessments (some examples: graded, ungraded, open-ended assessments; nonthreatening ones with no single right answers; written or oral assessments; those that make use of charts, graphs, or other forms, such as drama).
12. Illuminate gains.
13. Avoid making comparisons to other students.
14. Allow students the opportunity to fail and recover.

MEANS TO AN END

Assessments are generally most effective when they are used to diagnose students' strengths and weaknesses as opposed to simple documentation; when they are used to plan instruction, not just hold students accountable; when there are multiple indicators for the teacher to consider; and when they lead to more opportunities to learn, not just to record achievement levels. Assessments are a means to an end, not the end itself. The better able we are at strengthening the assessment profile of the students we teach, the better able we will be to teach these students. Without a strong assessment profile, our instructional efforts suffer the risk of being misguided. Unfortunately, the assessment profiles generated for our black male students have frequently not been complete enough. With a limited focus, many classroom teachers are unable to provide responsive instruction at all, or perhaps they manage to provide just temporary relief from reading difficulties—for example, when test preparation is the focus, which can lead to marginal gains on standard assessments that students do not sustain over the years.

Up to now, I have discussed the theoretical and the instructional strands needed for creating nesting grounds to advance the literacy of black males. Support, however, is often needed as teachers work to incorporate these strands into their teaching. They need time, ongoing reflection, and support; they need ongoing professional development.

CHAPTER 10

ESTABLISHING A PROFESSIONAL-DEVELOPMENT COMMUNITY

A cathedral of this magnificence cannot be built without people believing in it so deeply and so truly that their beliefs become contagious.

A prerequisite of building out and up is to begin by digging down deep and within.

Bill Shore, *The Cathedral Within*

Three yeas ago, I purchased a digital camera and began to take pictures of cathedrals in Buffalo, New York. I continue to take pictures of cathedrals as I visit different locations throughout the United States. This love affair with cathedrals began after I read *The Cathedral Within* by Bill Shore (2001). I was particularly impressed by the two quotes that serve as the epigraphs of this chapter. At the time I read the book, I was providing professional-development support in an elementary school with a 100 percent black student population. It occurred to me that establishing a professional-development community is akin to building cathedrals. Such a community cannot be built without people believing in it so deeply and so truly that the belief becomes contagious. Building a professional-development community also requires some deep digging, particularly when the goal is to root out years of failure, a situation faced by many schools.

In this chapter, I describe the process of establishing a professional-development community, using principles I learned from my experiences in a Chicago elementary school and a Washington, D.C., high school. Each school had a high percentage of black students. In each setting, the achievement of the black male students was a particular concern. My goal in both schools was getting teachers to "franchise" an approach for improving reading achievement. I did not want the schools to feel like a Burger King, where teachers were doing things their own way. The goal was to establish one community—one franchise—while respecting the expertise and individual choice of teachers.

During a schoolwide staff development session in one of the schools, I shared a poem of mine with the teachers and administrators to emphasize the need for them all to become one community.

Grasping, pulling, not quite able to find the flow of the current.
The piranhas streaked in front of me—nearly escaping, I grasped for
    another day
Finding a different path; continuing with a similar stroke.
Two feet in front was an ordinary swimmer
Traveling an even keel I sought out his . . .
Then came a school of fish—multicolored, assorted
I lost sight of the path to fresh air;
now fearing a drown, I continued with a similar stroke
only to find that I was losing more ground.
Flapping faster, harder, as the piercing sun from above began to fade
Suffocating, and losing sight I was determined to refine my fineness
That I was accustomed to . . . and again passes another ordinary swimmer

Looking much like the first swimmer
who had a stroke deemed inferior to my superior stroke
one that I was not willing to abandon.
The hour was late and with shortening breaths
fearing death became my imminent domain
not quite ready to be food for worms or an undiscovered buried treasure
I released my extraordinary efforts for ordinary pursuits.

To my surprise, I began to rise with the current
Dashing seaweed and thin carp
My head now above the water I released my fears
and took a breath of fresh air.
Like the ordinary swimmers who perfected an ordinary stroke
I reached a shore that minutes before
seemed only to be a dream.

My intention in sharing this poem was to acknowledge that there are exceptional teachers in all schools, but that being exceptional is not enough to effect schoolwide change. I also wanted to make the point that teachers often hold on to things (a similar stroke) even when faced with evidence that things need to change. When ordinary swimmers perfect an ordinary stroke within a community of swimmers, the tide begins to rise for all. Success then becomes possible in situations where failure once seemed inevitable. In the end, the poem suggests that schools need ordinary teachers doing exceptional things.

Black men who succeed often feel fortunate that they got exceptional teachers. This was the case with me. My life might have turned out very differently if I was assigned to Room 205 instead of Room 202. The luck of the draw should not determine a student's fate. Schools need more than one or two exceptional teachers. They need a community of teachers focused on similar goals with administrative support to help them accomplish those goals.

Efforts are now being made throughout the United States to improve reading achievement in middle schools and high schools. Professional-development initiatives to encourage teachers to teach reading across the disciplines are part of these efforts. For the middle and high school teacher, teaching reading requires more than the knowledge of reading strategies. To be effective, teachers need to understand the developmental and cultural needs of their students. They also need to understand how classroom environments support or impede literacy learning. They also need to recognize that planning effective instruction for low-achieving English language learners may be quite different from planning instruction for native English speakers who are reading at grade level. Teachers may have to come up with different ways to discuss texts with students who resist education because they view a cultural disconnect between their home lives and the school environment. The discussions with these students may well be different from those conducted with students who find cultural similarities between their home and their school. Although each group of students requires high teacher expectations, the way to support students to achieve those expectations may be qualitatively different. Teachers who understand this are in a better position to plan literacy instruction that is responsive to the needs of all their students.

Establishing a professional-development community is not easy to do, but it is important. Creating learning opportunities and organizational structures that provide time for learning and setting them up in a way that improves reading throughout the school are also important. Schools can become storehouses of achievement when focused professional-development communities are established. The key is to identify the interrelated components of professional development that will result in a comprehensive focus on literacy that builds from year to year. Effective professional-development communities require effort in three broad categories—implementation, continuation, and evaluation.

IMPLEMENTATION

Establishing a strong conceptual basis for a professional-development community is a key to its success. Vibrant professional-development communities combine concrete, teacher-specific activities, ongoing and continuous assistance, and regular meetings with peers (Huberman and Miles 1984; Joyce and Showers 1988). The more complex the change, the more interaction during planning is needed. Teachers are more likely to change their behavior when they believe in and understand the change and can modify the ideas to work in their own classrooms (Schlechty 1990). Teachers and administrators not only want evidence that a recommended change works; they also want to see it work for the students for whom the change is being proposed. They also want to know how the change will affect them personally in terms of time and energy, and what the rewards are likely to be. Addressing these issues can offset some of the resistance people naturally feel when changes are proposed.

Professional-development approaches that focus on quick-fix solutions or that try to do too much with too little support are likely to fail. The necessary resources need to be available, as do individuals who are ready and qualified to give support when questions and concerns emerge. An effective professional-development community assumes that its members possess the ability and the desire to learn and are willing to take advantage of the opportunities provided. Adults should be respected for their prior knowledge and experiences.

CONTINUATION

Effective professional-development communities promote ongoing learning not just to individual teachers, but on a schoolwide basis (Smylie 1995). Such communities are sustained and focused, address the needs of students, and relate to plans for school improvement. It benefits the entire community when teachers observe in each other's classrooms, analyze one another's data, and report successes and failures to their professional-development group with the aim of helping individual students. Virginia Richardson (1994) found that when teachers engage in "elicitation and reconstruction" of their teaching process, they tend to rely less on external conditions to explain their teaching. In elicitation, teachers review some aspect of their instructional behavior and explain or justify that behavior with a "critical friend." Then, the teacher and the critical friend analyze the teacher's explanation and justification of the classroom behavior.

Leaders of professional-development communities need to find ways to sustain the culture of professional development. They can do this by passing on relevant information, by allowing teachers to participate in in-service training, by buying relevant professional journals, and by discussing interesting innovations at meetings and being very explicit in what is expected from teachers (Clement and Vandenberghe 2000).

Professional-development communities are most effective when they are collaborative, when they are grounded in the teachers' own work and in research on best practices, and when they provide teachers with opportunities to experiment and evaluate new ideas in the classroom. They become more important as they move toward long-term continuous learning in the context of the school and the classroom and with the support of colleagues (Lieberman 1995). Ralph Putnam and Hilda Borko (2000) have noted that professional development should provide opportunities for teachers to construct knowledge of subject matter and pedagogy in an environment that supports and encourages risk taking and reflection. The purpose of professional-development communities should not rest on the implementation of a specific innovation or policy, but focus on creating individual and organizational habits and structures that make continuous learning a valued part of the culture of schools and teaching (Fullan 1990). Professional development should also translate into visible changes in student academic performance and behavior.

EVALUATION

Carol Lyons and Gay Su Pinnell (2001) identified student achievement and changes in teaching as two major categories for evaluating professional development. They contend that an effective professional-development system includes systematic monitoring of its impact and assert that the bottom line is whether or not changes are taking place in the classroom. To assess progress in a systematic way, these authors suggest that the professional developer ask at minimum four questions:

1. How is the group working together?
2. What kinds of changes are taking place in practice?
3. What impact are the changes having on students?
4. What can be learned from the professional development?

All the participants must be involved in the evaluation to encourage ownership of the professional-development process and content. These evaluations should be conducted regularly and be part of the discussions among the participants that are intended to reinforce the overall aims and the hoped-for changes. Many professional-development programs fail because follow-up evaluation occurs too infrequently (Fullan 1990). Michael Fullan contends that all those involved should incorporate the attributes of high-quality professional development in as many activities as possible. This includes the evaluation component.

I have found that a professional-development community can fail when there is no strong conceptual framework and when participation in the community is left to the discretion of individual teachers. It can also fail when the roles and responsibilities of the members of the community are not well defined and teachers are not provided with the support they need to execute their roles and responsibilities. In addition, professional-development communities that focus only on reading instruction for students of historically underperforming groups run the risk of failure because they fail to consider other variables—curriculum orientations, the role of literacy instruction—that have the potential to improve students' reading achievement.

DEVELOPING A REAL-LIFE COMMUNITY

In an effort to address the literacy needs of the black adolescent students in Chicago and Washington, D.C., professional-development communities were planned. Teachers needed help in reconceptualizing the role of literacy instruction for their students, eradicating ineffective and disempowering curriculum orientations, and learning how to use a culturally responsive approach to literacy teaching. The focus was to be on teachers' adopting a comprehensive framework of literacy teaching, learning to discuss texts responsively, and strengthening students' assessment profile. This led in turn to several conclusions:

1. The professional development needed to be anchored, with a clear purpose and with discussion of what factors could improve student achievement.
2. Teachers needed to be provided with the necessary physical resources and materials for instructing students.
3. Any approach that did not lead to observable differences in teachers' and students' behaviors would be resisted.
4. A consistent professional-development plan and timetable needed to be established.

A five-day summer institute was held to help the teachers establish a strong conceptual basis for the professional-development community and to get them to rally around a comprehensive framework of literacy teaching. Discussions of various strategies for word study, fluency, read-alouds, comprehension, and writing were planned. One of the goals of the summer institute was to get the teachers to reconceptualize the role of their literacy instruction. Two central themes were how to teach students reading in the midst of turmoil and how to create nesting grounds for struggling readers. Participants were given handouts to help them reconceptualize their role.

I began by giving participants a visual depiction of the living conditions of African Americans in communities similar to the one in which the

school was located. The pictures I showed depicted environmental conditions that led to violence, hopelessness, despair, and ultimately death for
many black young people. The pictures conveyed to the teachers the idea
that the environment students find themselves in outside of school affects
what happens in school. After the show of pictures, I asked the teachers if
they believed that impoverished black children born in abject conditions
could be educated to compete in this society; if they believed that they
could provide education that would allow students to enter a different discourse (Gee 1989) from the one in which they were born; and if they
believed there are poor black children so affixed to their status that they
cannot escape. These questions served as a focus in my direct work with
the teachers as I helped them shape a professional-development community. The teachers would encounter these questions repeatedly, in various
settings—in individual conferences, in grade-level meetings, in schoolwide
staff-development sessions, and in many of the professional readings they
were given.

The reconceptualization of literacy instruction that was a focus of the
institute was carried through into the teachers' practice. During a grade-
level meeting I had with two of the teachers six months after the summer
institute, one of them described how she and a student of hers were
engaged in a battle of wills the day before. The teacher told me, "I said 'I
don't know who you are meeting after school,' but she told me that if she
was not out of here at ten minutes to three she was going to leave regard-
less. I told her if she walked out of that door without my permission, I
would write her up. That was the only reason she stayed. . . . We eventually ended when I told her how much I loved her and I cared about her
and I was sorry she got involved in that gang situation."

This teacher's remarks gave us a chance to revisit some of the themes
of the institute. After the teacher had finished telling us her story, I said to
her, "If you remember this summer, I mentioned reading amidst turmoil;
that's what this is really about. I continue to say that we have to worry
about more than the intellectual part of our kids; it's the emotional part
that should concern us as well. A lot of teachers can learn to teach the
reading strategies. But we have to ask, 'Why am I teaching this?' Or 'What
type of material am I going to use?' I think for us this is really important.
How do we design and structure our curriculum? We want curriculum
moments. The curriculum moments won't solve all of our problems, but
we want curriculum moments to bring out different discussions. That's
really the most important part of our jobs. . . . We have to be honest with
ourselves to say that everything we do in class will not change their lives

. . . but at least we're not going to shuck and jive and BS them about stuff that's really unimportant and insignificant."

The meeting continued as the two teachers described the things that were working during their lessons. The teacher who had told of her confrontation with a student mentioned using Dick Gregory's novel *Nigger*, and how she focused on the skill and strategies of identifying dynamic and static character traits. She also described how the book had been useful for mending the relationship with the student who had confronted her a day earlier. "We started reading *Nigger* by Dick Gregory," she said, adding, "The person I had a confrontation with yesterday ordinarily does not like to read out loud. But today she did such a beautiful reading and the class clapped for her. . . . They enjoy the book and we have been having a lot of discussions."

I said to her, "That's the primary reason I brought in some of the books. I am hoping that from *Nigger,* and *Holes* [Sachar 1998], which the other class is reading, that the students are able to identify that Brother Dick Gregory went through some struggles or identify with some of the struggles in *Holes*."

The conversation at this grade-level meeting typifies many of those that took place during professional-development sessions in both Chicago and Washington. The conversations highlighted the role that literacy instruction could and should serve for the seventh- and eighth-grade students in the Chicago school as well as for the older students in the Washington, D.C., high school.

In both schools, establishing a healthy professional-development community required materials and processes to support the implementation of a comprehensive literacy framework. The materials included student and teacher materials; the processes included individual post-observation conferences, grade-level meetings, and schoolwide staff development sessions.

MATERIALS

At the sites where I worked to help establish a professional-development community, I made sure that teachers were provided with curriculum materials to support student learning and professional readings to support their own professional development. I gave them novels to consider using with their students. A large percentage of these, like the other curriculum materials I presented, were written by African American authors or had African American characters. I selected the materials with an eye to helping students better understand historical changes, substantiate their existence, and help them prepare for the future. I also selected materials that could be used to move students to honor their own presence, "a powerful demanding presence not limiting the space in which the self can roam" (Achebe 1988, p. 53). Many of the curriculum materials described earlier in this book were used with the teachers in Chicago and Washington.

It is also important to their development that teachers read professional materials that will help them improve their ability to teach black adolescents. Passing on relevant information is one of the ways to sustain the culture of professional development (Clement and Vanderberge 2000). Therefore, I made sure that professional readings in the form of articles, book chapters, and entire books were given to teachers in the schools. Materials were selected to reinforce information presented during individual post-observation conferences, grade-level meetings, and schoolwide staff development sessions. Important details in the selections were underlined beforehand to encourage the teachers to read them. After all, I was well aware that there are a great many things competing for a teacher's time. Figure 10.1 is a list of professional readings I shared with the seventh- and eighth-grade teachers in Chicago.

PROCESSES

Collaboration among teachers and administrators and leaders of the professional-development community is necessary, and administrators must plan organizational structures that support educators' professional growth and that focus on the goals of the professional-development community. Four effective organizational structures were put into place in the schools where I provided professional-development support.

Individual Post-Observation Conferences

Using a model suggested by Alan Reiman and Lois Thies-Sprinthall (1999), our individual post-observation conferences began with a conversation about the teacher's feelings about the lesson under discussion. Then we talked about learning outcomes, classroom management, the teacher's behavior and focus, and upcoming lessons. In most cases, I sat down with individual teachers for a conference within forty-eight hours of the lesson.

The teachers understood that I was looking for several things when I visited their classrooms: the implementation of the literacy framework;

PROFESSIONAL READINGS

Baker, M. 2002. "Reading Resistance in Middle School: What Can Be Done?" *Journal of Adolescent and Adult Literacy* 45 (5): 364–366.

Colvin, C., and L. Schlosser. 1998. "Developing Academic Confidence to Build Literacy: What Teachers Can Do." *Journal of Adolescent and Adult Literacy* 41 (4): 272–281.

Delpit, L. 1995. "Education in a Multicultural Society: Our Future's Greatest Challenge." In *Other People's Children* (pp. 167–183). New York: New York Press.

Foster, M., and T. B. Peele. 1999. "Teaching Black Males: Lessons from the Experts." In V. Polite and J. Davis, eds., *African American Males in School and Society: Practices and Policies for Effective Education* (pp. 8–19). New York: Teachers College Press.

Fountas, I., and G. S. Pinnell. 1996. "What Is Guided Reading." In *Guided Reading* (pp. 1–10). Portsmouth, NH: Heinemann.

Harvey, S., and A. Goudvis. 2000. "Questioning." In *Strategies That Work: Teaching Comprehension to Enhance Understanding* (pp. 81–94). Portland, ME: Stenhouse.

Harvey, S., and A. Goudvis. 2000. "Strategy Instruction and Practice." In *Strategies That Work: Teaching Comprehension to Enhance Understanding* (pp. 27–41). Portland, ME: Stenhouse.

Ivey, G., and K. Broaddus. 2001. "'Just Plain Reading': A Survey of What Makes Students Want to Read in Middle School Classrooms." *Reading Research Quarterly* 36 (4): 350–377.

Ladson-Billings, G. 1992. "Reading Between the Lines and Beyond the Pages: A Culturally Relevant Approach to Literacy Teaching." *Theory into Practice* 31: 312–320.

Ladson-Billings, G. 1994. *The Dreamkeepers: Successful Teachers of African American Children.* San Francisco: Jossey-Bass.

Moore, D., T. Bean, D. Birdyshaw, and J. Rycik. 1999. "Adolescent Literacy: A Position Statement." *Journal of Adolescent and Adult Literacy* 43 (1): 97–111.

Rosenbaum, C. 2001. "A Word Map for Middle School: A Tool for Effective Vocabulary Instruction." *Journal of Adolescent and Adult Literacy* 45 (1): 44–49.

Tatum, A. W. 2000. "Against Marginalization and Criminal Reading Curriculum Standards for African American Adolescents in Low-Level Tracks: A Retrospective of Baldwin's Essay." *Journal of Adolescent and Adult Literacy* 43 (6): 570–572.

Tatum, A. W. 2000. "Breaking Down Barriers That Disenfranchise African American Adolescent Readers in Low-Level Tracks." *Journal of Adolescent and Adult Literacy* 44 (1): 52–64.

Tatum, A. W. 2002. "Nesting Ground." *Principal Leadership* 2 (1): 26–32.

Tovani, C. 2000. *I Read It, but I Don't Get It.* Portland, ME: Stenhouse.

Weir, C. 1998. "Using Embedded Questions to Jump-Start Metacognition in Middle School Remedial Readers." *Journal of Adolescent and Adult Literacy* 41 (6): 458–467.

Woodson, C. G. 2000. *The Mis-education of the Negro.* Chicago: African American Images.

FIGURE 10.1 Professional Readings

characteristics of a classroom environment that supported adolescents; instruction and assessment practices; and curriculum choices. I generally used four questions to generate conversation:

1. How did you feel about the lesson?
2. What things are going particularly well?
3. Do you have any major concerns at this point?
4. What can I do to support you?

Specific literacy behaviors of the students (including the student's degree of participation, miscues, refusal to read aloud or silently, and comprehension responses) were always the focus of the post-observation conferences. I always tried to structure the conferences in a way that fostered authentic discussion about students' literacy behaviors and focused on ways to help students.

Grade-Level or Departmental Meetings

Grade-level or departmental meetings took several forms. Sometimes they were used to introduce instructional approaches. I would discuss the role of literacy instruction for black students in an attempt to get the teachers to reconceptualize their literacy instruction, as reflected, for example, in the meeting I had with the two teachers described earlier in this chapter. The meetings were also used to discuss the content of the professional readings the teachers were given. In addition, we also used meetings to address concerns relevant to an adolescent student population.

The grade-level or departmental meetings were an important vehicle for addressing issues of professional-development support that could not be accomplished in other settings. Here teachers could discuss how different strategies actually worked in their classrooms. They could share insights and offer advice for handling certain student behaviors or problems. Most important, in these meetings the teachers had the opportunity to discuss their teaching behaviors with peers and adopt practices that their fellow teachers had successfully implemented. The grade-level or departmental meetings were critical to sustaining the momentum of the community's professional-development efforts. The meetings reminded the teachers that they were not fighting their battles alone; their peers were wrestling with some of the same issues.

Schoolwide Staff-Development Sessions

Effective professional development promotes ongoing learning on a schoolwide basis (Smylie 1995). Schoolwide staff-development sessions were conducted to model lessons using the literacy framework, extend what occurred in the teachers' classrooms, share assessment data collected across grades and departments, and encourage collective efforts to increase the reading achievement of black students. These sessions gave participants the opportunity to communicate across grade levels and departments and got teachers involved in literacy activities that required collaboration. The schoolwide staff-development sessions placed professional development in a larger context. As one teacher told me, "I'll never forget one of your things with your staff development sessions: you always wanted to know what was the teacher's focus. What is your focus? Because if you don't have a focus, what the hell are you doing?"

ADDRESSING THE NEEDS OF BLACK MALES

In order to establish professional-development communities to address the needs of black adolescent males, professional-development planners must identify individuals who understand adolescent literacy, understand effective approaches for educating black students, and understand effective professional-development practices for teachers. Too often, the deliverers of professional development understand research-based instructional approaches, but cannot explain how these approaches fit with other considerations for advancing students' literacy. Establishing professional-development communities must stretch beyond finding the "right" instructional strategies and programs and getting teachers to follow them.

Several principals and district leaders have asked my opinion about certain strategies and their effectiveness in improving schoolwide reading achievement. Recently, a school's leadership team asked me what I thought about using K-W-L charts as an approach to improve reading in the content areas. They were planning to place their bets on a single instructional approach to address the literacy needs of their high school students, many of whom were poor and black. Others have asked me what I thought about commercial professional-development packages that provide both training and materials for the training. My response is always the same. Such strategies, by themselves, will do little to improve schoolwide reading achievement. I recommend establishing a professional-development community that revolves around the theoretical and instructional strands offered in this book. I also recommend that they pay attention to current research on effective professional-development practices. Taking this approach improves the chance of advancing the literacy not only of black males, but of all students.

CHAPTER 11

CONDUCTING TEACHER INQUIRIES

It becomes very difficult to take the risk of going into the desert to begin to irrigate the land, to begin to grow what you need, and be able to shear the lamb and get the wool to make what you need to wear.

We have to go into the desert. In the desert the only way we can succeed is to have faith in what has already made us who we are.

Na'im Akbar, *Visions for Black Men*

n this chapter, I discuss the final strand for creating nesting grounds where the literacy of black adolescent males can flourish: conducting teacher inquiries. As you were reading the previous chapters, several questions may have occurred to you. For example, you may have asked:

- Why do we need to give special attention to the literacy of black males?
- How can I increase the standardized test scores of black males?
- How can I use the texts I am required to use to address the turmoil black males experience?
- What texts should I use to empower my black male students?
- How do I address the needs of black male students in a diverse classroom?
- How can I become a culturally responsive teacher?
- Why are my black male students resisting my instruction?
- How can I get the black males in my class to read the texts recommended in this book when they are struggling with decoding?
- How can I teach my black male students in the ways suggested here when the school administration is not supportive?
- How do I motivate my black male students?
- How does my literacy instruction affect the young men in my class who are ready to surrender their life's chances before they come to believe in their life's choices?
- How can I close the reading achievement gap between low performance and excellence that many black males experience?
- What are some research-based reading strategies that work with black male students?

These are the questions teachers and school administrators ask time and time again when considering approaches to improve the reading achievement of their black male students. I am always struck by the last question. During a telephone conversation with a high school administrator, I was asked to provide a list of publications on teaching reading to black males. In reply, I began to tell him about the need to combine the theoretical and instructional strands described throughout this book. I also mentioned the need to provide professional-development support for his teachers and told him that I would send him some articles on all of these issues. He responded, "Yes, that would be great, but please send me some articles on research-based reading strategies that work with black males." His question implied that there are different research-based reading strategies for black males than there are for other groups. The fact is, *there are no black-male-only research-based reading strategies*. The reading strategies are the same for all students; how students are taught and in what contexts are what make a difference. "How and in what contexts should we teach the research-based reading strategies?" would have been a more appropriate question for this administrator to ask.

Like many of my colleagues, I am seeking answers to the questions listed earlier. I began to seek answers to some of these questions early in my teaching. As Na'im Akbar suggests in this chapter's epigraph, I had to go to the desert and irrigate the land to begin to grow what I needed to address the literacy needs of black males. I also had to have faith that I could succeed in teaching *all* my students. After all, teaching all children was the reason I decided to become a teacher. My focus on black males specifically began with a single, specific question: *Why are those four black boys refusing to read in my class?* The question is not as general as the ones earlier; it related specifically to what I was observing every day in my classroom. I could not rely on an outside expert to answer this question. I had to systematically pay attention to what was going on in my classroom. I decided to conduct my own inquiry. In the end, this helped me identify the barriers that disenfranchised my students (Tatum 2000).

Conducting one's own inquiry is a powerful way to discover the approaches to teaching that are most effective with black males. Nancy Dana and Diane Silva (2003) define teacher inquiry as a systematic, intentional study of one's own professional practice. They add:

> *Inquiring professionals seek out change by reflecting on their practice. They do this by posing questions or "wonderings," collecting data to gain insights into their wonderings, analyzing the data along with reading relevant literature, making changes in practice based on new understandings developed during inquiry, and sharing findings with others.* (p. 7)

My own inquiry started with a question, a notebook, a tape recorder, a desire to be a successful teacher of all students, and four young men. I asked the young men to join me for conversation during my designated planning periods and while the other students attended art, music, or gym.

During our first conversation, I laid the truth before them: "Man, I cannot figure out how to get you guys to read in my class. I need you to help me out." I can still see their faces. They began to look at each other with expressions that meant, "What is this man talking about?"—but they said nothing. Finally I spoke again. "Why aren't you guys reading in my class?" With the tape recorder playing, one of the young men said, "Mr. Tatum, we are not used to this stuff. It's like we're starting over again in eighth grade." The other three boys nodded their heads in agreement, then added their own comments:

"You expect us to know these big words and snap your fingers at us to make sure we say them within one second."

"We never read novels before."

"Our teachers expected us to fail so we didn't do the work."

The most striking comment was from one of the young men, who confided, "You just don't know—we discuss the stuff you talk about during the lesson outside of the class; we just don't talk about it in the class."

I began to reflect on the students' comments as I listened to the recordings. I realized that these young men were interested in the materials, but that they did not have the working tools, the confidence, or the experience to fulfill the expectations I held for them. These young men clued me in that I needed to help build their vocabularies. They suggested that I needed to support them through our reading of novels. They implied that I needed to find a way to bring their discussions into the classroom. They also communicated that they pay attention to teacher expectations. These young men provided me with powerful insights.

I began recording my daily reflections in a journal for approximately four months. I recorded miscues from the students' oral readings. I reflected on their level of participation, noticing such things as who asked questions and who offered comments. I recorded my feelings about how various lessons had succeeded or not, focusing on my performance—my successes and failures. I recorded my impressions of how well students worked in groups. I recorded how they responded to different forms of assessments. I collected samples of their writing. It was important to record my thoughts and reflect on them throughout the inquiry, as it enabled me to assess changes in my teaching and my students' literacy behaviors. It also allowed me to revisit my earlier thinking to see if it was changing over time and to chart my professional growth. Recording my changes in thoughts and efforts also enabled me to communicate my findings with others who were wrestling with similar issues.

As a result of the ongoing weekly conversations with my students, I began to reshape my teaching. I began to invite my students into the instructional and assessment process. I gave them a chance to assess my teaching every five weeks. I would ask these, or some variation of these, questions:

1. What part of my teaching do you find most useful in helping you become a better reader?
2. What part of my teaching is least useful in helping you becoming a better reader?
3. What would you recommend that I continue doing?
4. What would you recommend that I stop right now?

Asking these questions gave me a direct line into my students' reading lives. I was able to gather information from them about the cognitive dimension of reading (for example, the benefits of a cloze activity, decoding multisyllabic words) as well as about the affective dimensions of reading (for example, the type of books they like, the type of activities they like). But I needed more information. I began to seek out professional literature to help me respond to my students' needs. I subscribed to professional reading journals and began to search educational publishers' Web sites for books. I also began to talk to colleagues and school administrators about my discoveries to gather their insights.

Teacher inquiry, which is sometimes referred to as action research, opens up a realm of possibilities for addressing the literacy needs of all students. Teacher inquiry highlights the role classroom teachers play as knowledge generators. It focuses on the concerns of teachers—rather than outside researchers—and engages teachers in the design, data collection, and interpretation of data around their questions (Dana and Silva 2003). Conducting inquiries allows teachers to understand their teaching more fully. It also allows teachers to come to know their students' literacy behavior more fully. Teachers become empowered by conducting inquiries and becoming reflective practitioners.

According to Geoffrey Mills (2003), teacher inquiry, or action research, can be used to:

■ Investigate a relevant classroom problem.
■ Expand the teacher's professional knowledge in a specific discipline.
■ Improve the teacher's practice, solve a problem, institute change, or enhance development.

Mills notes that teacher reflection is part of each step of the inquiry process, and that inquiry involves a cyclical process of planning, acting, and reflecting. Conducting teacher inquiries has several benefits. It enables teachers to improve student learning, to enhance their own teaching, and to integrate theory and practice. The challenge is committing the time and energy to teacher inquiry so that it does not feel like an add-on, but an integral part of one's teaching. At the core of teacher inquiry is professional self-improvement (Freebody 2003).

Teacher inquiry can be particularly important for our black male students. Teachers who work with these young men each day are well positioned to ask questions that are central to teaching them. These teachers are well positioned to try new approaches and reflect on issues in a classroom or school setting. They are well positioned to bridge the separation between theory and action. Most important, teachers of black males have a voice that needs to be heard, particularly when they are able to successfully teach these young men. Too often, the voices of classroom teachers are marginalized in the discussion about what works with black males. Their expertise is too often unacknowledged.

Conducting inquiries enabled me to discover how to address the literacy needs of my black male students. It allowed me to improve my teaching. It helped my young men become better readers and writers. It led me to identify the theoretical, instructional, and professional-development strands described throughout this book. I believe, however, that more inquiries are needed, and that administrators must encourage and support teachers in this endeavor. Some questions that inquiries could address include the following:

- How can culturally relevant trade books be used to teach in the content areas?
- How can the voices of black males be effectively engaged in the assessment process?
- Which research-based strategies do black adolescent males find most useful in helping them become better readers?
- What effect does cooperative grouping have on black adolescent males' reading of lengthy texts?
- What factors are preventing black adolescent males from engaging in reading and writing activities?
- How can writing be used to increase black males' interest in reading?
- What happens to the literacy behaviors of black adolescent males when they are given the choice of a wide range of reading materials?
- What effect does a schoolwide professional-development plan have on the reading achievement of black adolescent males?
- How can technology be used to support the literacy development of black adolescent males?

- How do black adolescent males respond to novels with black male characters?
- How can current events be used to advance the literacy of black adolescent males?

The inquiry questions that can be asked are innumerable. Some of the inquiries I have suggested can be conducted in one classroom or across classrooms. They can be conducted across several time frames—a single semester or an entire school year. Determining how best to conduct the inquiry depends on the question being asked. For example, inquiries on the impact of cooperative grouping on black adolescent males' reading of lengthy texts and on using culturally relevant trade books can be conducted in a shorter time frame than one on the effect a schoolwide professional-development plan has on increasing the reading achievement of black males.

Teacher inquiries hold a great deal of promise because teaching is a dynamic process. Advancing students' various forms of literacy is imbued with complexities. Adolescents have shifting identities. Culture, economics, and gender can influence educational outcomes. Racism and classism still exist in the United States. This is the broader ecology and educational backdrop affecting the literacy of black adolescent males who suffer from academic underperformance. There is no simple solution; one method cannot fix all that needs to be fixed. But I believe that if classrooms become nesting grounds, and if teachers use the various strands I have outlined in these pages to help create these nesting grounds, the literacy of their black male students will flourish.

TWO
ASSESSMENT
FORMS

HIP-HOP IT, CAN'T STOP IT

Name: _____

1. (Think and Search Question) Changes in rap over the past thirty years have included
    a.   less anger and less marketing
    b.   more anger and less marketing
    c.   more anger and more marketing
    d.   no anger and no marketing

2. (Word Study) *Notable moments* refer to
    a.   minor events
    b.   happy events
    c.   yearly events
    d.   important events

3. (Comprehension) Place the following on the time line that follows to show rap music's evolution.
    a.   presence of female rappers
    b.   product marketing
    c.   street-corner sessions
    d.   rap on television
    e.   million- and multimillion-dollar rap ventures
    f.   presence of white rappers
    g.   mixing poetry with beats
    h.   connection between rap and violence

4. (Short Answer—Constructed Response) How has rap changed over time? How has it remained the same?

5. (On-Your-Own Question) How is the evolution of music similar to the evolution of human life? (You can create your own rap or short poem to answer this question.)

DESIGNER GENE WARFARE

Name: _____ Score: ____%   Grade: A B C D F

Reading Strategies (1/2 point each)
1. Which of the following is true about answering comprehension questions?
   a. If the text has the same wording as the questions then the answer will more than likely be true.
   b. There should be evidence in the text to support the answer.
   c. The key is to focus on the words of the text.
   d. None of these are true.
2. When marking and annotating text it is important to
   a. underline all the facts.
   b. use highlighter.
   c. use chapter objectives, self-constructed questions, and questions at the end of the chapter as a guide.
   d. both *b* and *c*.
3. You should never make up your own questions prior to reading because they can only cause confusion.
   a. True
   b. False
4. The best way to understand a textbook is to just begin reading.
   a. True
   b. False

Vocabulary Development (1/2 point each)
Match each of the following words with its definition.
1. acquiesce ___
2. condescend ___
3. hypothetical ___
4. patronize ___
5. tentative ___

a. conditional, probationary
b. to deal with, to buy from
c. to comply passively, to agree
d. to stoop to someone's level
e. uncertain, unproven

Define the underlined words:
1. With recombinant DNA technology, it is now possible to develop a nearly underlined variety.
   a. limited   b. deadly   c. unlimited   d. designed
2. Potent toxins until now were available only in minute quantities.
   a. short period of time   b. large   c. small   d. dangerous
3. This genotypical makeup predisposes them to certain diseases.
   a. slants   b. shows   c. prevents   d. eliminates
4. They can be employed in many diverse settings.
   a. strange   b. unique   c. various   d. cheap

(continued on next page)

DESIGNER GENE WARFARE (CONTINUED)

Comprehension Questions

Use textual references to support your responses.

1. (1 point) The author is writing this selection to
    a. describe the effects of genetic research.
    b. explain the different types of biological warfare.
    c. discuss a new threat to humanity, its potential effects, and how it has come about.
    d. clear up misconceptions about potentially deadly viruses.
2. (2 points) What does the author mean by "the rapid exploitation of nature's resources for warfare purposes in ways not even imagined ten to fifteen years ago" (on page 92)?
    a. Nature is being destroyed for the wrong reasons.
    b. Elements of nature are now being used for evil due to advances in science and technology.
    c. Nature is now dangerous because of misguided researchers who want to destroy it.
    d. People are quickly taking advantage of all the good in nature to prepare for war.
3. (2 points) What makes biological warfare a greater threat than traditional forms of war with soldiers and military hardware (guns, tanks, bombs, etc.)?
    a. It is difficult for richer nations to protect themselves against biological warfare, which gives poorer nations a greater advantage.
    b. It requires less expertise and can be developed in diverse settings.
    c. The effects of biological warfare can last longer and there is no way to call an end to it.
    d. Biological warfare will kill more people.
4. (2 points) Which of the following is a true statement about biological warfare and designer genes?
    a. Biological warfare and designer genes are the same thing.
    b. Biological warfare makes possible the creation of designer genes.
    c. Designer genes make possible the creation of biological warfare.
    d. Biological warfare and designer genes can be inserted into microorganisms.
5. (3 points) Referring to the article, list three things that make designer genes a significant threat if used for warfare.
    a.
    b.
    c.

Short Answers

6. (2 points) How can new engineering technologies provide a versatile form of weaponry? List at least two ways.
7. (1 point) What did the author want you to understand after reading this essay?

REFERENCES

Achebe, C. 1988. *Hopes and Impediments*. New York: Doubleday.

African American Literature: Voices in a Tradition. 1998. New York: Holt Rinehart & Winston.

Akbar, N. 1992. *Visions for Black Men*. Tallahassee, FL: Mind Productions & Associates.

Allington, R., and P. Cunningham. 1996. *Schools That Work: Where All Children Learn to Read and Write*. New York: Addison Wesley Longman.

Alvermann, D. 1998. "Imagining the Possibilities." In D. Alvermann, K. Hinchman, D. Moore, S. Phelps, and D. Waff, eds., *Reconceptualizing the Literacies in Adolescent Lives*, pp. 353–372. Mahwah, NJ: Lawrence Erlbaum.

Apple, M. 1990. *Ideology and Curriculum,* 2nd ed. New York: Routledge.

Au, K. 1993. *Literacy Instruction in Multicultural Settings*. Fort Worth, TX: Harcourt Brace Jovanovich.

Baldwin, J. 1953. *Go Tell It on the Mountain*. New York: Laurel.

———. 1995. *The Fire Next Time*. New York: Modern Library Edition.

Brooks, G. 1994. *Blacks*. Chicago: Third World Press.

Brozo, W. 2002. *To Be a Boy, To Be a Reader: Engaging Teen and Preteen Boys in Active Literacy*. Newark, DE: International Reading Association.

Butterworth, E. 1992. *Discover the Power Within You*. New York: HarperCollins.

Campbell, J., P. Donahue, C. Reese, and G. Phillips. 1996. *National Assessment of Educational Progress 1994 Reading Report Card for the Nation and States*. Washington, DC: National Center for Education Statistics, U.S. Department of Education.

Carson, B. 1992. *Think Big: Unleashing Your Potential for Excellence*. New York: HarperPaperbacks.

Carter, R. 2003. *The Sixteenth Round: From Number 1 Contender to Number 45472.* London: Penguin Global.

Cellblocks or Classrooms? The Funding of Higher Education and Corrections and Its Impact on African American Men. 2002. Washington, DC: Justice Policy Institute.

Chubb, J., and T. Loveless. 2002. *Bridging the Achievement Gap.* Washington, DC: Brookings Institution Press.

Clement, M., and R. Vandenberghe. 2000. "How School Leaders Can Promote Teachers' Professional Development: An Account for the Field." Paper presented at the Annual Meeting of the American Educational Research Association, New Orleans.

Collins, C. J. 1993. "A Tool for Change: Young Adult Literature in the Lives of Young Adult African Americans." *Library Trends* 41 (3): 378–392.

Collins, M. 1982. *Marva Collins' Way: Returning to Excellence in Education.* Los Angeles: Tarcher.

Connor, M. K. 2003. *What Is Cool? Understanding Black Manhood in America.* Chicago: Agate.

Corwin, M. 2001. *And Still We Rise: The Trials and Triumphs of Twelve Gifted Inner-City Students.* New York: Perennial.

Cose, E. 2002. *The Envy of the World: On Being a Black Man in America.* New York: Washington Square Press.

Csikszentmihalyi, M. 1990. *Flow: The Psychology of Optimal Experience.* New York: Harper and Row.

Cushman, K. 1995. *The Midwife's Apprentice.* New York: HarperTrophy.

Dana, N., and D. Silva. 2003. *The Reflective Teacher's Guide to Action Research: Learning to Teach and Teaching to Learn Through Classroom Inquiry.* Thousand Oaks, CA: Corwin Press.

Darling-Hammond, L. 1998. "New Standards, Old Inequalities: The Current Challenge for African American Education." In L. Daniels, ed., *The State of Black America,* pp. 109–171. New York: National Urban League.

Davis, S., G. Jenkins, R. Hunt, and L. Page. 2002. *The Pact: Three Young Men Make a Promise and Fulfill a Dream.* New York: Riverhead Books.

Dostoevsky, F. 1971. *The Adolescent.* New York: W. W. Norton & Company.

Douglass, F. 2001. *The Narrative of the Life of Frederick Douglass, An American Slave.* New Haven, CT: Yale University Press.

Du Bois, W. E. B. 2001. *The Education of Black People: Ten Critiques, 1906–1960.* New York: Monthly Review Press.

Dyson, M. E. 2001. *Holler If You Hear Me: Searching for Tupac Shakur.* New York: Basic Civitas Books.

———. 2004. *The Michael Eric Dyson Reader.* New York: Basic Civitas Books.

Ellison, R. 1947. *Invisible Man.* New York: Random House.

Epstein, D., J. Elwood, V. Hey, and J. Maw, eds. 2001. *Failing Boys? Issues in Gender and Achievement.* Buckingham, England: Open University Press.

Fanon, F. 1967. *Black Skin, White Masks.* New York: Grove Press.

Faulkner, W. 1995. *Collected Stories of William Faulkner.* New York: Vintage.

Foster, M. 1997. *Black Teachers on Teaching.* New York: New Press.

Franklin, A. 2004. *From Brotherhood to Manhood: How Black Men Rescue Their Relationships and Dreams from the Invisibility Syndrome.* Hoboken, NJ: John Wiley & Sons.

Freebody, P. 2003. *Qualitative Research in Education: Interaction and Practice.* Thousand Oaks, CA: Sage.

Friedman, T. 2000. *The Lexus and the Olive Tree.* New York: Anchor Books.

Fullan, M. 1990. "Staff Development, Innovation, and Institutional Development." In B. Joyce, ed., *School Culture Through Staff Development,* pp. 3–25. Alexandria, VA: Association of Supervision and Curriculum Development.

Galbraith, J. K. 1996. *The Good Society: The Humane Agenda.* Boston: Mariner Books.

Gay, G. 2000. *Culturally Responsive Teaching: Theory, Research, and Practice.* New York: Teachers College Press.

Gee, J. 1989. "Literacy, Discourse, and Linguistics: Introduction." *Journal of Education* 17: 5–17.

Gilbert, R., and P. Gilbert. 1998. *Masculinity Goes to School.* New York: Routledge.

Goodman, J. 1994. *Stories of Scottsboro.* New York: Vintage.

Graham, L. O. 2000. *Our Kind of People: Inside America's Black Upper Class.* New York: Perennial.

Gregory, D. 1995. *Nigger: An Autobiography.* New York: Pocket Books.

———. 2001. *Callus on My Soul: A Memoir.* Atlanta: Longstreet Press.

Grossman, K. 2004. "Shape Up This Year, or Else, State Tells 22 Chicago Schools." *Chicago Sun-Times,* August 18, p. A4.

Hale, J. 1994. *Unbank the Fire: Visions for the Education of African American Children.* Baltimore: John Hopkins Press.

Haley, A., and Malcolm X. 1965. *The Autobiography of Malcolm X.* New York: Ballantine Books.

Hamilton, V. 1990. *Cousins.* New York: Scholastic.

Hansberry, L. 1959. *A Raisin in the Sun.* New York: Random House.

Harding, V. 1981. *There Is a River: The Black Struggle for Freedom in America.* New York: Harcourt Brace & Company.

Harris, V. 1993. *Teaching Multicultural Literature.* Norwood, MA: Christopher-Gordon.

Hawkins, J. 1990. "The Cries of My Ancestors: The Uncomfortable Story of Slavery Must Be Told Honestly." *Teacher* (June/July): 8–9.

Henry, A. 1998. "'Speaking Up' and 'Speaking Out': Examining 'Voice' in a Reading/Writing Program with Adolescent African Caribbean Girls." *Journal of Literacy Research* 30 (2): 233–252.

Herbert, B. 2001. "In America: On the Way to Nowhere." *The New York Times,* p. A15.

Herbert, T. K. 1995. "Inviting and Respecting Real Response." In. B. Livdahl, K. Smart, J. Wallman, T. Herbert, D. Geiger, and J. Anderson, eds., *Stories from Response-Centered Classrooms,* pp. 49–63. New York: Teachers College Press.

Hollins, E. R. 1996. *Culture in School Learning: Revealing the Deep Meanings.* Mahwah, NJ: Erlbaum.

hooks, b. 2004. *We Real Cool: Black Men and Masculinity.* New York: Routledge.

Huberman, A., and M. Miles. 1984. "Rethinking the Quest for School Improvement: Some Findings from the DESSI Study." *Teachers College Record* 86: 34–54.

Hudley, C. 1995. "Assessing the Impact of Separate Schooling for African American Male Adolescents." *Journal of Early Adolescence* 15: 38–57.

Ivey, G. 1999. "A Multicase Study in the Middle School: Complexities Among Young Adolescent Readers." *Reading Research Quarterly* 34: 172–192.

Jones, L., L. Newman, and D. Isay. 1998. *Our America: Life and Death on the Southside of Chicago.* New York: Simon & Schuster.

Joyce, B., and B. Showers. 1988. *Student Achievement Through Staff Development.* New York: Longman.

King, J., and C. Mitchell. 1990. *Black Mothers to Sons: Juxtaposing African American Literature with Social Practice.* New York: Peter Lang.

Kitwana, B. 2002. *The Hip Hop Generation: Young Blacks and the Crisis in African-American Culture.* New York: Basic Civitas Books.

Kliebard, H. 1995. *The Struggle for the American Curriculum,* 2nd ed. New York: Routledge.

Kotlowitz, A. 1991. *There Are No Children Here: The Story of Two Boys Growing Up in the Other America.* New York: Anchor Books.

Kunjufu, J. 1995. *Countering the Conspiracy to Destroy Black Boys.* Chicago: Third World Press.

Ladson-Billings, G. 1994. *The Dreamkeepers: Successul Teachers of African American Children.* San Francisco: Jossey-Bass.

———. 2002. "I Ain't Writin' Nuttin': Permission to Fail and Demands to Succeed in Urban Classrooms." In L. Delpit and J. Dowdy, eds., *The Skin That We Speak: Thoughts on Language and Culture in the Classroom,* pp. 107–120. New York: New Press.

Lieberman, A. 1995. "Practices That Support Teacher Development." *Phi Delta Kappan* 76: 591–595.

Lipman, P. 1995. "'Bringing Out the Best in Them': The Contribution of Culturally Relevant Teachers in Educational Reform." *Theory into Practice* 34: 202–208.

Loof, S. 2001. "'Dr. Death' to Testify in Apartheid-Era Trial." *The St. Petersburg Times,* July 24.

Lowry, L. 1989. *Number the Stars.* New York: Yearling.

———. 1993. *The Giver.* New York: Yearling.

Lynch, W. 1712. Speech on Slave Control Delivered in Jamestown, Virginia. Available online: www.blackspeak.com/speeches/slavecontrol.htm.

Lyons, C., and G. S. Pinnell. 2001. *Systems for Change in Literacy Education: A Guide to Professional Development.* Portsmouth, NH: Heinemann.

Mahiri, J. 1998. *Shooting for Excellence: African American and Youth Culture in New Century Schools.* New York: Teachers College Press.

———. 2004. *What They Don't Learn in School: Literacy in the Lives of Urban Youth.* New York: Lang.

Majors, R., and J. Gordon. 1993. *The American Black Male: His Present Status and His Future.* Lanham, MD: Rowan & Littlefield.

Mathabane, M. 1986. *Kaffir Boy: The True Story of a Black Youth's Coming of Age in Apartheid South Africa.* New York: Plume.

Maynard, T. 2002. *Boys and Literacy: Exploring the Issues.* New York: Routledge.

McCall, N. 1995. *Makes Me Wanna Holler: A Young Black Man in America.* New York: Vintage Books.

McLaughlin, M., M. Irby, and J. Langman. 1994. *Urban Sanctuaries: Neighborhood Organizations in the Lives and Futures of Inner-City Youth.* San Francisco: Jossey-Bass.

Mills, G. 2003. *Action Research: A Guide for the Teacher Researcher,* 2nd ed. Columbus, OH: Merrill Prentice Hall.

Mosley, W. 2000. *Workin' on the Chain Gang: Shaking off the Dead Hand of History.* New York: Ballantine Books.

Myers, W. 1995. *The Glory Field.* New York: Scholastic.

———. 1999. *Monster.* New York: HarperTempest.

———. 2001. *The Greatest.* New York: Scholastic.

———. 2003. *The Beast.* New York: Scholastic.

National Institute of Child Health and Human Development. 2000. *Report of the National Reading Panel: Teaching Children to Read: An Evidence-Based Assessment of the Scientific Literature on Reading and Its Implications for Reading Instruction.* NIH Publication No. 00-4769.

Newkirk, T. 2002. *Misreading Masculinity: Boys, Literacy, and Popular Culture.* Portsmouth, NH: Heinemann.

Nieto, S. 1999. *The Light in Their Eyes: Creating Multicultural Learning Communities.* New York: Teachers College Press.

Nobles, W. 1987. "Psychometrics and African American Reality: A Question of Cultural Antimony." *Negro Educational Review* 38 (3): 45–55.

Obidah, J. 1998. "Black-Mystory: Literate Currency in Everyday Schooling." In D. Alvermann, K. Hinchman, D. Moore, S. Phelps, and D. Watt, eds., *Reconceptualizing the Literacies in Adolescents' Lives,* pp. 51–71. Mahwah, NJ: Lawrence Erlbaum Associates.

Ogbu, J. 1998. "Voluntary and Involuntary Minorities: A Cultural-Ecological Theory of School Performance with Some Implications for Education." *Anthropology and Education Quarterly* 29: 155–188.

Pierce, C. 1970. "Offensive Mechanisms." In F. Barbour, ed., *The Black Seventies.* Boston: Porter Sargent Publisher.

Polite, V., and J. Davis. 1999. *African American Males in School and Society: Practices and Policies for Effective Education.* New York: Teachers College Press.

Putnam, R., and H. Borko. 2000. "What Do New Views of Knowledge and Thinking Have to Say About Research on Teacher Learning?" *Educational Researcher* 29: 4–15.

Raphael, T. 1986. "Teaching Question Answer Relationships, Revisited." *Reading Teacher* 39: 516–522.

Reiman, A., and L. Thies-Sprinthall. 1999. *Mentoring and Supervision for Teacher Development.* New York: Longman.

Richardson, V. 1994. *Teacher Change and the Staff Development Process: A Case of Reading Instruction.* New York: Teachers College Press.

Rifkin, J. 1995. *The End of Work: The Decline of the Global Labor Force and the Dawn of the Post-Market Era.* New York: Putnam.

Rowan, L., M. Knobel, C. Bigum, and C. Lankshear. 2001. *Boys, Literacies and Schooling: The Dangerous Territories of Gender-Based Literacy Reform.* Philadelphia: Open University Press.

Sachar, L. 1998. *Holes.* New York: Yearling.

Schlechty, P. 1990. *Schools for the Twenty-First Century.* San Francisco: Jossey-Bass.

Shore, B. 2001. *The Cathedral Within: Transforming Your Life by Giving Something Back.* New York: Random House.

Smith, M., and J. Wilhelm. 2002. *Reading Don't Fix No Chevys: Literacy in the Lives of Young Men.* Portsmouth, NH: Heinemann.

Smylie, M. 1995. "Teaching Learning in the Workplace." In T. R. Guskey and M. Huberman, eds., *Professional Development in Education: New Paradigms and Practices,* pp. 92–113. New York: Teachers College Press.

Suskind, R. 1999. *A Hope in the Unseen: An American Odyssey from the Inner City to the Ivy League.* New York: Random House.

Takaki, R. 1990. *Iron Cages: Race and Culture in Nineteenth-Century America.* New York: Oxford University Press.

Tatum, A. W. 2000. "Breaking Down Barriers That Disenfranchise African American Adolescent Readers in Low-Level Tracks." *Journal of Adolescent and Adult Literacy* 44 (1): 52–64.

———. 2003. "Advancing the Literacies of African American Adolescents: A Case Study of Professional Development." Ph. D. diss., University of Illinois–Chicago.

———. 2004. "A Roadmap for Reading Specialists Entering Schools Without Exemplary Reading Programs: Seven Quick Lessons." *Reading Teacher* 58 (1): 28–39.

Taylor, M. D. 1976. *Roll of Thunder, Hear My Cry.* New York: Dial.

Walker, D. 1965. *Appeal: To the Coloured Citizens of the World, but in Particular, and Very Expressly, to Those of the United States of America.* New York: Hill and Wang.

Washington, B. T. 1901. *Up from Slavery.* New York: Doubleday.

Watson, C., and G. Smitherman. 1996. *Educating African American Males: Detroit's Malcolm X Academy.* Chicago: Third World Press.

Weir, C. 1998. "Using Embedded Questions to Jumpstart Metacognition in Middle School Remedial Readers." *Journal of Adolescent and Adult Literacy* 41: 458–467.

White, J., and J. Cones. 1999. *Black Man Emerging: Facing the Past and Seizing a Future in America.* New York: Routledge.

Wilhelm, J. 1997. *"You Gotta Be the Book": Teaching Engaged and Reflective Reading with Adolescents.* New York: Teachers College Press.

Wolff, T. 2003. *Old School.* New York: Knopf.

Woodson, C. G. 1933. *The Miseducation of the Negro.* Washington, DC: Associated Publishers.

Wright, R. 1945. *Black Boy: A Record of Childhood and Youth.* New York: HarperPerennial.

———. 1993. *Native Son.* New York: HarperPerennial.